The Express Guides

The Express and Kogan Page have joined forces to publish a series of practical guides offering no-nonsense advice on a wide range of financial, legal and business topics.

Whether you want to manage your money better, make more money, get a new business idea off the ground – and make sure it's legal – there's an Express Guide for you.

Titles published so far are:

Great Ideas for Making Money
Niki Chesworth

Your Money
How to Make the Most of it
Niki Chesworth

Buying a Property Abroad
Niki Chesworth

You and the Law
A Simple Guide to All Your Legal Problems (Second edition)
Susan Singleton

How to Cut Your Tax Bill Without Breaking the Law
(Fourth edition)
Grant Thornton, Chartered Accountants

Be Your Own Boss
How to Set Up a Successful Small Business
(Second edition)
David McMullan

Readymade Business Letters That Get Results (Second edition)
Jim Douglas

The Woman's Guide to Finance
How to Manage All Your Money Matters
(Second edition)
Tony Levene

Buying Your First Franchise
G R Clarke

Your Home Office
A Practical Guide to Using Technology Successfully (Revised second edition)
Peter Chatterton

How to Sell More
A Guide for Small Business
(Second edition)
Neil Johnson

Investment Guide
Practical Advice for Making the Right Choice (Second edition)
Tony Levene

Network Marketing
An Introductory Guide
David Barber

How to Cope with Separation and Divorce (Second edition)
David Green

Available from all good bookshops, or to obtain further information please contact the publishers at the address below:

Kogan Page Ltd
120 Pentonville Rd
London N1 9JN
Tel: 0171 278 0433
Fax: 0171 837 6348

THE EXPRESS

YOU AND THE LAW

*A guide to dealing with
your legal problems*

SECOND EDITION

SUSAN SINGLETON

KOGAN
PAGE

**To my husband, Martin, and our children,
Rachel, Rebecca and Benjamin**

First published in 1994

Kogan Page Limited
120 Pentonville Road
London N1 9JN

© E S Singleton 1997

British Library Cataloguing in Publication Data
A CIP record for this book is available from the British Library.

ISBN 0 7494 2488 5

Typeset by Saxon Graphics Ltd, Derby
Printed and bound in Great Britain by Clays Ltd, St Ives plc.

Contents

1
The law

Introduction

The law affects us all. Although the majority of people will manage to go through life without ever appearing in the dock for a criminal offence, few are able to avoid the law altogether. Birth, marriage, divorce, buying a house, evading tax and losing your job all involve the law. This book covers most of the main legal areas relevant to the average person. It aims to give the reader basic information about these.

The law frightens many people; not just through fear of imprisonment and the police, but also the complexity, mystique and cost of the legal system in England and Wales. This book seeks to explain the complexities, and reveals that many of the main legal concepts, laws and other rules are really quite simple. It attempts to sweep away some of the mystique of the law, which is fostered by forbidding, archaic costumes, wigs and gowns, and fuelled by unnecessary legal jargon, clung to by a largely self-perpetuating, white, middle-class legal profession, although this image has begun to change.

Going to law is expensive. Few people are entitled to Legal Aid, and even fewer have the resources to fund lengthy and expensive litigation. In many ways, access to justice is restricted to the very rich and the very poor. There are many millions in the middle who cannot afford to enforce their rights. This book gives advice on where to go for legal advice, free and otherwise, and how to keep the costs down.

All societies, however primitive, have laws regulating the behaviour of their citizens. Laws are primarily there to help and protect members of society. Laws set out formally the rights and obligations which we enjoy in relation to our fellow human beings. The UK does not have a written constitution setting out basic human rights, but all sorts of statutes give rights to citizens, in addition to imposing obligations, such as to refrain from criminal activities, to pay tax, provide for our children and spouse, drive with care and wear seat belts in cars.

The more complicated the society, the more detailed the laws need to be. Today, in Britain, not only are basic laws forbidding murder and theft necessary, but also criminal statutes prohibiting fraud and computer hacking, as well as a whole range of other sophisticated, modern offences.   .

Laws address criminal behaviour and activities, but most law-abiding citizens only have contact with what is known as 'civil' law, the law dealing with negligence, breach of contract, transfer of property and divorce. Some actions will involve both criminal and civil offences. For example, if you punch someone in the nose, not only have you committed a criminal offence for which the police could bring proceedings, and for which a fine or jail sentence might be appropriate, but also you could be sued for the civil wrong or 'tort' of trespass to the person.

This book gives guidance on the law of England and Wales. Although many laws apply throughout the rest of the UK, some do not, so always seek advice from a local lawyer. The system of law in Scotland, for example, is different from that in England.

Some legal terms explained

A section on Legal Terms, at the back of this book, contains a list of the most commonly used legal phrases and their meanings. However, it will be difficult to get the most from this book unless certain legal words are explained here.

Plaintiff When legal proceedings are brought, ie someone is sued, the person or company bringing the action, issuing the writ or starting the proceedings off, is known as the plaintiff.

Defendant The individual or company which is sued and, therefore, has to defend the action is known as the defendant.

Solicitor A solicitor is the lawyer you will see for legal advice, who has passed the Law Society's professional examinations and completed practical training, called in full a 'solicitor of the Supreme Court'.

Barrister A barrister is a lawyer who is a specialist in advocacy (speaking in court), who has been called to the Bar by one of the Inns of Court and passed the barristers' professional examinations. Your solicitor will instruct a barrister to represent you in court proceedings, but you are unlikely to have much contact with barristers in seeking legal advice. The legal profession is split in two, divided between solicitors and barristers, both of which are known as lawyers.

Writ A judicial writ is issued to bring legal proceedings. Civil cases are started in the courts by the issuing and serving of a writ (either by posting or hand delivery), an official-looking document, completed by the solicitor or individual bringing the action and issued by the court.

Litigant in person A litigant is someone who is bringing legal proceedings or suing, ie litigating. A litigant in person is an individual who chooses to represent themselves in court, rather than having a barrister act on their behalf.

Damages Civil claims in the courts are for damages, which is money claimed from the defendant to compensate the plaintiff for loss arising from the action or default of the defendant. For example, if the defendant sells the plaintiff a product which explodes and damages the plaintiff's house, the plaintiff may sue the defendant for damages to compensate him or her for the loss suffered.

The courts

Criminal cases are handled either in the magistrates' court or the Crown Court, though all criminal cases must start out in the magistrates' courts. The magistrates' courts deal with the vast majority of criminal cases in England and Wales, and each court is comprised of lay or stipendiary magistrates. Lay magistrates are not lawyers and undertake the work on a voluntary basis. Stipendiary magistrates are usually solicitors and are salaried.

The Crown Courts handle more serious criminal offences, such as murder and appeals from magistrates' courts decisions. The Crown Court is presided over by a High Court judge, sitting with a jury when trying criminal cases.

Legal cases which do not involve criminal offences, ie what are known as 'civil' proceedings, may be handled by a variety of courts depending on the case. The magistrates' courts handle a mixture of family law matters, such as adoption and maintenance orders.

Actions for damages and other civil suits are brought in the county court, presided over by a circuit judge for cases involving large sums of money or a district judge for smaller matters. More important cases still will be heard in the High Court, which is divided into a number of divisions, depending on the nature of the case being heard.

There are other bodies, too, which provide a forum for the resolution of legal disputes, such as industrial tribunals for employment disputes, and some legal disputes are arbitrated.

Finally, there are courts of appeal. Appeal from the magistrates' courts in criminal cases is to the Crown Court, and from there to the Court of Appeal, Criminal Division and finally the House of Lords. For civil cases the appeal court is the Court of Appeal and from there the House of Lords.

However, the aim of this book is to help you to avoid going to court and only to litigate as a last resort. There are cases, of course, where the only way to extract payment or obtain redress is through a court action, but it is cheaper, simpler and quicker to resolve disputes amicably.

This book contains checklists to enable the reader picking up the book in a crisis to find the answer or suggested course of action to be taken in a variety of legal emergencies. What it cannot do is give specific legal advice nor be comprehensive. Each of the legal topics covered in this book is the subject of individual, lengthy legal textbooks. The book sets out an outline of the law in the relevant legal area and individual legal advice should always be sought for particular cases. The book gives the reader a basic understanding of a series of legal areas, which should make any legal advice obtained easier to understand, but should not be used as a substitute for obtaining legal advice.

2
Getting help

When faced with a legal crisis the first port of call is the solicitor. However, solicitors are not the only source of legal advice. This chapter looks at the different sources of advice available and considers the respective merits of each for particular types of legal requirements. Addresses for the various bodies mentioned are given at the end of the book, in Sources of Further Information.

Solicitors

Used to dealing with a wide range of legal problems, solicitors are generally the best people to advise in relation to legal matters. Regulated by the Law Society, solicitors are required to comply with a strict code of conduct to protect the client. They must not be interested, or involved, in the matter in dispute and, as 'solicitors of the Supreme Court', they are required to comply with high professional conduct standards. Solicitors must take out compulsory indemnity insurance to compensate the client if they give negligent advice and the profession also runs a 'compensation fund' for those who suffer at the hands of the unscrupulous solicitor. Solicitors train for at least six years before they qualify.

All these standards and insurances do not come cheap, and there can be no doubt that solicitors are generally regarded as expensive, though perhaps not when comparing the cost of an emergency plumber against the average of £300 charged by a solicitor to convey a house over a period of months or the approximate sum of £70 to draw up a will.

So, when should a solicitor be used, assuming that unlimited funds are not available? A solicitor should be used for the following, though, in law, the individual (but not a limited company) is always entitled to represent him or herself, if they choose to do so:

- moving house;
- getting divorced;
- getting arrested;
- other complex legal matters, such as nuisance or negligence claims.

What solicitors cost

Never use a solicitor, whatever the circumstances, without obtaining an estimate of their likely charges first. Most firms of solicitors are familiar with giving estimates these days. Ensure that the estimate is in writing and that it is clear what it covers. Most solicitors now issue a 'client engagement letter' to new clients, as required by their professional conduct rules, which should indicate the basis for charging. If your chosen solicitor does not deal with charging in his or her first letter to you, then raise the issue yourself. If you were buying a car or engaging a roofing contractor you would find out the likely cost first. Going to law should be no different. Indeed, given the speed with which legal costs can escalate it is often more important than in many other areas of life to obtain estimates.

The solicitors' charges will principally be based on the amount of time which they need to spend on the matter. The longer the job takes, the more it will cost you. However, time 'costs' are not the only factor relevant to charging. The solicitor will also look at the complexity of the matter, whether a partner or junior employee undertook the work, the value of the transaction and its importance to you, as well as a number of other factors.

If a solicitor you have chosen refuses to give any indication of cost, try someone else. However, this is not to say that the cheapest will be best. You are paying for quality of advice and the better, more expert firms employ better qualified staff who earn higher salaries.

What the cost will be will depend on the matter and the firm instructed. Many firms of solicitors charge about £80 per hour plus VAT, though the large specialist practices will have charging rates of £150 or even, in central London, rates of £250 per hour and over. It is often possible to obtain an estimate for a straightforward transaction such as moving house or having a will written. For more complex disputes, where it is not clear how long the matter will take, an estimate to give preliminary advice may be all the solicitor can give. If the firm has substantial experience of legal matters of the sort with which you are concerned, they ought to have some experience of what they have charged others in the past. Ask them. Except for certain limited categories of case, like personal injury claims, solicitors are not allowed to charge for litigation (contentious) cases on a no win/no fee basis.

Choosing the right firm

The best way to choose a solicitor is to find one whom a friend has used successfully in the past. There is little to beat a personal recommendation. However, ensure that the firm has experience of the type of case upon which you need advice. These days most solicitors specialise. Most high street practices, however, will have solicitors who undertake conveyancing or deal with the most common criminal and contract disputes. There should be little difficulty in finding a practice which can handle the mainstream cases, but if you have a personal injury dispute or an employment law problem, or any other specialist type of case, find a firm which specialises in that work.

Either contact acquaintances who have had similar legal problems or ask the firms you contact what their experience is of the type of matter in hand. Ask how many such disputes they have handled before. There are legal directories which list firms by their specialisation, details of some of which appear in Sources of Further Information, and firms of solicitors appear in the *Yellow Pages* and also advertise in local newspapers.

Hints on using a solicitor

Solicitors are meticulous, obsessively interested in detail and keen to have everything in writing. They need to be. Bear this in mind in instructing a law firm. Give them copies of all relevant documents and write them comprehensive, but clear letters. Remember that the more you contact the solicitor the more you are likely to be charged. Every time you telephone, most solicitors will enter the length of the call in a book or on a computer system, which will regurgitate the time spent when the next bill is produced. Time is definitely money, so:

- pass all information on at the beginning;
- do not pester the solicitor too often, but ask for regular progress reports to be sent to you;
- respond to requests for information from the solicitor promptly;
- require an initial estimate and notification when costs reach the level of the estimate.

If you do not understand what the solicitor has said, do not be embarrassed and pretend that you have. You are paying for the advice and if you do not understand it is the solicitor who is at fault. Ask for a simpler explanation.

Above all, aim for a friendly, but professional, working relationship. Expect high standards. If you are unhappy you are within your rights to terminate your contract or 'retainer' with the solicitor and change firms. In appropriate cases you may be able to sue the solicitor and/or report him or her to the Office for the Supervision of Solicitors (OSS) or the Legal Services Ombudsman, where the standard of service has not been good enough.

Other sources of legal advice

There is no legal requirement to use a solicitor and it may be that free legal advice is available. Law centres operate in many urban areas, often funded by the local authority. They often offer free advice, specialising in areas such as welfare and housing law. Citizens' Advice Bureaux offer free advice around the country on many legal areas and other advice centres operate, sometimes staffed by solicitors on a rota basis, opening in the evenings and offering free advice. Not all these bodies will be able to take on a full legal case, but they will be able to give valuable initial advice. In particular, they should be able to advise you as to whether or not it is worth your pursuing a matter further with a solicitor.

Some bodies, such as the Consumers' Association, offer advice in particular specialist fields and specific complaints against companies operating in a number of different industries may be capable of investigation by trade associations representing the relevant industry or by the various ombudsmen. Finally, your house contents insurers may offer a free legal helpline or you may have legal expenses insurance. Your trade union or professional body may similarly assist or back your case.

Legal Aid

Finally, for those with little disposable income, free legal advice from solicitors may be available under the hard-pressed Legal Aid scheme. Even those who do not qualify for Legal Aid may be able to attend a first fixed-fee interview with a solicitor, which many firms operate.

Legal Aid comes in a number of different forms, but for most people the most important point is the very low income limits which apply. Under the so-called 'Green Form' scheme for legal advice and assistance on criminal and civil matters, two hours of advice can be given free in many areas, including divorce and drafting documents. Where disposable capital exceeds £1000 or disposable income is more than £77 per week, the Green Form cannot be used.

Full blown, civil Legal Aid may be available if a means and a merits test is passed. Disposable capital should be under £6750 per annum and disposable income under £7595 per annum before Legal Aid will be available. Only those with capital of less than £3000 and income less than £2563 per annum have all their legal costs paid under the scheme. Those on income support are automatically eligible. If you win your case but not your costs and you have legal aid, the money due to your solicitor and barrister is taken off the money (or other property) you win as damages in the case under the 'statutory charge'. Legal Aid is therefore a form of loan.

There are similar tests for criminal Legal Aid, where those with capital under £3000 and income of £49 or less per week, receive full criminal legal aid. Those earning above the limits, where they are eligible at all, must make a contribution to the costs. Those requiring advice on arrest at a police station may be able to obtain free legal advice under the 'duty solicitor' scheme. Limits change, so always check the latest figures.

For most people Legal Aid is not available. For straightforward legal matters a solicitor can be used and the costs minimised using the steps set out in this chapter. Seeking free advice from a law or advice centre or Citizens' Advice Bureau can either reduce the cost burden or remove it entirely.

Summary — getting help

Free legal advice

- Law Centre — Details in Sources of Further Information

- Advice centre — Look in *Yellow Pages*
- Citizens' Advice Bureau — Local paper
  Call local council

- Your trade union — Union head office

- Specialist agencies such as Consumers' Association, government bodies DoE, DSS, DTI, OFT etc — Details in Sources of Further Information *Yellow Pages*

- Ombudsmen and trade associations — Details in Sources of Further Information

- Local council (May offer general advice) — *Yellow Pages*

- Legal Aid (But note low income and capital requirements) — From solicitors which offer Legal Aid
  See *Yellow Pages*, local press, high street offices

- Duty solicitor — Available on rota basis at police station

Buying legal advice

- Solicitors (May offer fixed price first interview) — Personal recommendation
  Specialist directories, see Sources of Further Information
  Local paper and *Yellow Pages*

3
Resolving disputes and taking legal action

Introduction

Not every contact with the law involves a dispute, but much of the business of law is a question of settling disagreements, whether in the context of divorce, arguments with neighbours or suing for debts owed. If you feel you need to take legal action against a person or company, always try to resolve the matter amicably first.

Establish the facts. Is there really a dispute at all? Could you be in the wrong? Everyone can be guilty of obstinately thinking that they are in the right. Look at the matter from the point of view of the other party. If this is too difficult for you, ask a dispassionate friend for their views in confidence. In some disputes there are justified complaints on both sides, and the matter can be amicably resolved with a bit of give and take on each side.

It is rarely financially justified to fight a hopeless or difficult case. Take advice and bury your pride, where necessary, though it is every- one's right to spend money fighting for a matter of principle.

If you have decided there is a genuine dispute, there are a number of different ways to settle it. First, try approaching the other party. Good communication is often the key to resolving disputes. Do your homework thoroughly. Check the facts and paperwork a number of times. For example, if you believe that you are owed money, have full details of the contract and all invoices, as well as details of reminders which have been sent.

Frequently disputes which have gone on for some time become stuck in a repetitive groove with each party simply reiterating their entrenched position. Recognise that there may need to be movement or compromise on each side before a dispute can be settled. Decide what is your 'bottom line' or final position.

Often a bit of psychology helps. Making the other person feel respected and appreciated, and showing an understanding of their point of view, even if you dislike them intensely and think their stance is wholly without foundation, gives them the chance to agree a settlement without losing face. If you offer some sort of apology, such as 'I am sorry we have reached this position. Perhaps I am to blame for not understanding your position. I know we would each like to put this dispute behind us, so should we settle for £300?', can result in a quicker, cheaper settlement than each party instructing solicitors and sending each other endless threatening letters.

Formal mediation and ADR

Where such informal attempts to settle disputes are not getting anywhere and the claim is not worth the expense of going to solicitors, then increasingly companies and individuals are turning to 'alternative dispute resolution', ADR or mediation. This covers a wide range of possibilities, including going to a mediator or expert to determine which party is in the right. You would have to pay the mediator, though.

When to sue

In Chapter 5 guidance is given as to how to go about bringing legal proceedings without a solicitor and what technical steps need to be taken to prosecute a case yourself. The most difficult question, however, is how to decide whether it is worth going to court or not. Ask yourself the following questions.

- Do you have a clear-cut case, such as a debt owed, or are there strong arguments in your opponent's favour which could prolong the dispute?
- What do unbiased friends or colleagues think of your case?
- What is the value of your claim? If it is very small, unless you are prepared to sacrifice money for principles, consider abandoning the case, though not until you have made a thorough nuisance of yourself, with hard-hitting letters and frequent telephone calls to try to extract compensation without going as far as bringing legal proceedings.
- What figure do solicitors estimate their costs to be for handling

your potential claim? Estimates are free and most solicitors are prepared to give them, so always obtain several.

What it costs to sue and recovering legal costs

There is no set scale of legal costs. Indeed, solicitors are free to charge whatever the market will stand. There are so many different types of legal claim that no useful list can be produced. The best way to ascertain the likely costs is to explain all the relevant facts to a solicitor and obtain an estimate, preferably in writing. There will be few legal cases where the costs will be under £100, so very small claims are virtually never going to be worth pursuing through the courts with the assistance of a solicitor unless you qualify for Legal Aid.

Some complicated claims will involve many hours of solicitors' time and will costs hundreds, if not thousands, of pounds. Remember, though, that you will be able to recover *some*, but not all, of your legal costs from the defendant if the case goes in your favour. However, the converse is also true. If you lose, and you should always remember that possibility, then you will have to bear a substantial proportion of your opponent's costs, unless the judge orders otherwise.

So, even if you choose not to use a solicitor and conduct the case yourself as a 'litigant in person', you may still have legal costs to pay, if you lose and are obliged to pay your opponent's costs. Some companies make much of this risk in forcing individuals to settle cases, threatening them with huge legal bills if the case is pursued and the party suing loses. Although this is certainly a real risk, where you are advised, preferably by a legal expert, that you have a very good case, that risk may well be worth running.

Where the case proceeds to a successful conclusion, the amount of legal costs which you can recover will vary. Usually the 'standard' basis of assessment is used and the party which wins is able to recover 'reasonable' costs from the other side. Sometimes an order by the court for costs is made on the 'indemnity' basis, although the same reasonableness test applies, but the successful plaintiff's views on what is 'reasonable' are given greater weight. A much greater proportion of the costs can be recovered on the indemnity basis.

Payments into court

During the course of a legal action the defendant may pay a sum of money 'into court', representing the amount of money for which the defendant would settle. If the case proceeds and the plaintiff wins less than that sum, then the defendant will not have to pay the plaintiff's costs. Always consider carefully whether or not to accept a payment into court, taking legal advice wherever possible, as the consequences of rejecting such a payment could be a Pyrrhic victory – you win the case but can recover no costs. If your costs exceed the damages which you win, all you have as consolation is moral vindication, which does not pay the bills.

Damages

Damages is the money which is won in compensation from the defendant. The judge in the dispute will make the order as to damages, which will usually comprise the sum of money necessary to place the plaintiff in the same position as if the defendant had not undertaken the wrongful action. So, for example, if the defendant has not paid for goods, the damages will be the sum due plus interest.

There is an obligation to 'mitigate' loss, which means that you should take reasonable steps to reduce your loss where possible. For example, in determining compensation in employment disputes, the court will look at what steps the dismissed employee has taken to find replacement employment. The plaintiff cannot sit back for the rest of his or her life and expect to be paid the salary they would otherwise have received had they not been dismissed.

Damages can also be reduced where the plaintiff is at fault. For example, in an action for negligence, where the plaintiff has added to his or her personal injury, for example, by acting recklessly on the road, which was partly the cause of a third party knocking them over, then the damages will be reduced by the judge to reflect the respective responsibility of the parties.

Timing

Court actions can be slow. However, this very much depends on the nature of the dispute. In cases of emergency it is possible to obtain 'injunctions' within a matter of days, restraining a company or individual from undertaking a particular activity pending the final trial. Most disputes, though, take months to go through the court procedure. Although there are strict time limits for filing a defence and proceeding with the formal stages of an action, the process is lengthy. You may not want to be involved in time-consuming and perhaps personally distressing litigation over a long period of time. Consider the personal, emotional and financial burden when deciding whether to sue.

Above all, be firm, but reasonable, in litigation or threatened litigation. It is worth stressing again that you should avoid going to court if alternative ways of achieving a settlement are possible, but where you have a good case and the costs are unlikely to exceed the claim, then sue.

4
Being sued

Action plan on receiving a writ or summons

A summons or writ arrives through the post. What should you do? Do not put it away or tear it up. If you do not serve a defence, for example, within a certain period, a judgment will be entered against you and the bailiffs may turn up to dispose of your possessions. The action you should take depends on the type of action which has been brought against you, but the following points should be considered.

- Check to whom the document is addressed. It may be meant for someone else. If it is, forward it to the addressee or return it to the sender.
- Read it carefully. If you cannot understand it, discuss it with someone who does, but not in a month's time when you know you will be speaking to a particular colleague or friend who is familiar with such things. Legal proceedings are serious, and should be considered and dealt with urgently.
- Note any time limits which appear on the document. Ring some local solicitors and ask for cost estimates for giving you some general advice on how to deal with the claim and ask how quickly you could see them for advice.
- Do not panic. Particularly for those who have rarely had contact with the courts, the procedure, documents and formality are frightening. However, panicking is not going to help. Sit down and calmly read the document through.
- Write a short description of what you think the document is all about and what action by what dates it requires you to take. If you have a pocket diary write down the time limits and deadlines in it straight away.

- Although it is important to act quickly, do take some time to consider the matter. Do not be frightened to such an extent that you foolishly decide to agree with the claim made against you in the legal document, even though you may have a very good case for refuting the allegations.

What form the action will take from receipt of the first writ or other legal document very much depends on what the case is about. Later chapters give information on specific legal areas. The major division between types of legal action is between 'civil' cases and 'criminal' cases. Most people are aware of the basic criminal offences, including such matters as driving offences and assaults. Civil cases could involve your being sued for breach of contract, negligence or nuisance. The procedure will differ, depending on which type of proceedings has been initiated.

Procedure in criminal cases

A criminal case will be brought by the Crown Prosecution Service, instigated by the police. Chapter 13 looks at what to do if you are arrested. Criminal cases are begun either by an arrest or by a 'summons' issued by a magistrate for the police. The summons can be served on the accused by post. The summons will state when the accused must appear in court, though some offences, such as careless driving, permit a guilty plea by post. In those cases there will be no need to appear in court, but there will still be a criminal conviction. If you did not commit the offence then the postal procedure cannot be used for a 'not guilty' plea.

Most criminal offences involve attendance at court. Virtually all criminal cases are heard in the magistrates' court and all such cases begin there. Very serious offences, which are known as 'indictable' offences, must be tried in the Crown Court. For some offences, which are described as triable either way, a choice may be made.

On receiving a summons for a criminal action it is wise to visit a solicitor with all the paperwork, as much detail as possible about the offence and the circumstances in which it arose.

If you do not turn up in court as specified on the summons then the case may proceed in your absence and you could be found guilty. Ask your solicitor for a description of how the proceedings for the particular offence with which you are charged will proceed. Generally, the prosecution will put their case to the magistrates. Various witnesses will be called on behalf of the prosecution and then the defence. Proceedings will be concluded by each side making a short speech summarising their case, and the magistrates will give their verdict or decision and determine the sentence, where the accused is found guilty.

Compensation

Private prosecutions for criminal offences are possible, though if the police have decided not to prosecute there are probably good reasons, such as lack of evidence, which would also apply if an individual is bringing proceedings. Such prosecutions are rare, as the party bringing the proceedings could end up paying the legal costs of the other party where their case is not successful.

Civil actions may arise from a criminal prosecution by the Crown Prosecution Service. For example, if you are beaten up in the street, whether or not the offender is prosecuted by the police the perpetrator of the offence can be sued for damages. If the defendant has no means, ie is poor, then any such civil action is not worth while. Those who have suffered from a criminal act may be entitled to State compensation, as well as having a right to bring an action for damages against the offender, from the Criminal Injuries Compensation Authority (address in Sources of Further Information at the back of this book). Whenever an individual is injured through a criminal act, an enquiry should always be made of the Board as millions of pounds of compensation are paid out each year.

Civil procedure

Most civil proceedings are served by post on the defendant. It is necessary to return the acknowledgement of service form, which comes with the other papers, within the time limit set out, otherwise judgment may be entered against you. If you, therefore, ignore the proceedings, this makes matters very easy for the plaintiff. The plaintiff does not have to prove the case and can apply for 'judgment in default'. You may have a perfectly good defence. Use the opportunity to put your side of the story.

The next stage in legal proceedings consists of a statement of claim in the High Court or particulars of claim in the county court. The initial writ may have contained the statement of claim or this may be dispatched later. This gives all the details of the plaintiff's case.

Where the defendant is contesting the case a defence should be filed. Generally it is preferable if a solicitor and often a barrister is used to assist in the drafting of the defence. It is important that the defence denies all or part of the claim properly and sets out the details of the defence which the defendant proposes to use. It is difficult to change the defence later, though not impossible.

After the defence the plaintiff may serve a reply to the defence and the defendant may serve a counterclaim with the defence. This is a claim against the plaintiff. For example, if a plaintiff is suing a customer for failing to pay for goods supplied, the customer's defence may be that the goods were of poor quality, and that they caused the defendant substantial losses as the goods exploded and damaged carpeting. The claim for compensation for the damaged carpet would comprise the counterclaim. Sometimes the parties ask for 'further and better particulars' of a claim, if the various documents served are not clear enough.

These various documents, statement of claim, defence etc are known as 'pleadings'. The pleadings do not go on for ever. There comes a point when pleadings will 'close' and then the parties have to give 'discovery' of their documents to each other, within 14 days of the close of pleadings. Lists of the relevant documents upon which the parties are relying on their case are exchanged and inspection of those documents arranged.

Most civil cases do not reach court. Most are settled or agreed before the trial, often outside the door of the courtroom on the day fixed for the hearing. Those that proceed to trial will be heard either in the High Court or the county court, depending on the size of the sum in dispute, ie the value of the claim. The plaintiff opens the case and presents its evidence. The defendant responds. Both parties may call witnesses in presenting their case and both conclude with speeches summarising their case. Judgment may be reserved and handed down another day where the judge needs to consider the facts more carefully. In straightforward actions, however, the judgment will be given immediately.

Orders

Where an individual is found guilty of a criminal offence the sentence needs little explanation. There is little difficulty in understanding a fine or a jail sentence, or even a community service or probation order. For civil disputes the judgment may require the defendant to pay damages to the plaintiff or to restrain the defendant from carrying out a particular activity, such as creating a nuisance. The party which wins the case must set in motion the procedures necessary to enforce the judgment (if the defendant does not pay up) and has a number of different ways of enforcement including the following.

- Sending in the bailiffs to seize goods of the defendant to the value of the claim.
- Attachment of earnings, so that the sum ordered to be paid is deducted from the wages of the defendant before the wages are paid to the defendant by his or her employer.
- Charging orders, comprising a 'charge' (which is a bit like a mortgage) over the defendant's home or other property. If the defendant fails to make the payments due under the judgment, then the charging order can result in a forced sale of the property charged, with repayment of the plaintiff out of the proceeds of sale.
- Garnishee orders, such as orders over bank accounts or other money held by the defendant.

Summary — being sued

- If you are sued, do not panic. Follow the stages set out on pages 24–5.
- Seek legal advice.
- Stick to the time limits set out in the legal documents which you receive.
- Orders for enforcing judgment include bailiffs, attachment of earnings orders, charging orders over property and garnishee orders.

5
The 'do-it-yourself' legal action

This chapter shows you how to go about bringing a legal action yourself without the aid of a solicitor. It is always wisest to seek legal advice, but this is not always possible. Citizens' Advice Bureaux and law centres (see Sources of Further Information) will be able to guide you, free, through the maze of bringing, or defending yourself against, a legal action in more detail than is possible in a book. However, here is some basic guidance to get you started.

First, consider the points made in the previous two chapters. Do you really have a justified cause of action? Is the claim worth the time and effort of bringing legal proceedings? If you think that it is, then the first step is to send a letter before action.

The letter before action

There is no legal requirement to give the other party to a legal action one last chance to 'pay up or be sued', but it is wisest to do so. What you should not do is send the other party a whole series of such letters. If they do not come up with an offer of settlement after your first or second threat then go ahead and issue proceedings.

Your letter should be short and clear. There is no need to write pages and pages of complaint, couched in emotive language. There follows a sample letter before action in a sale of goods case. Assume that you bought a new washing machine which did not work. The company arranged to collect it and supply a replacement. They took the machine away, but have not sent a replacement nor have you had your money back. You have written to them on several occasions and now your patience has run out.

There are no special legal words which must be used in such letters. It is important that you do not admit your responsibility in any way for the dispute, otherwise your letter could be used against you later in

[your address]

[date — the day you
intend posting letter]

Mr/Ms ....
[job title]
The Shoddy Goods Co Ltd
[Address]

[Their reference]

Dear [   ],

*Washing Machine purchased on [[???]] at Shoddy Goods Store,
Blanktown, Model number 12345, serial number 2536475*

I refer to our previous correspondence in this matter, copies of
which are enclosed for your ease of reference. On ... 199.. I purchased the above washing machine, which was non-operational. As
you were unable to correct the fault you agreed to replace the
machine on ... 199.. On ... 199.. you collected my machine, but I
have received neither a replacement nor a refund of my money.

I am writing to inform you that unless I receive a duplicate
machine which works properly or a full refund of the sum of £...
which I paid for the machine within seven days of the date of this
letter, I shall issue legal proceedings against you for recovery of my
money costs, interest and damages.

Yours sincerely

[Your name]

Enc

any legal proceedings. If the matter comes to court you might also claim additional damages so do not suggest you will be claiming nothing more. Perhaps you have had to make trips to the launderette or the machine may have damaged your kitchen walls and floor when it broke down. Obviously the earlier you claim all items of loss the better.

Make sure that you set out the facts clearly and include all relevant details. It may seem a nuisance to have to refer to previous letters for dates and reference numbers, and go to the trouble of photocopying letters, but it is essential to ensure that the letter is fully comprehensive and that you give all the information necessary. Get it typed.

Ensure that the letter is addressed to a named individual. If you are not sure to whom you should write at a company, for example, telephone them first. When someone receives a letter addressed to them in person they are more likely to deal with it. If the letter is addressed very generally it could be passed around a large company for weeks, if not months, before someone cannot avoid being delegated with the task of dealing with it.

Make sure that you post the letter on the date which appears on the letter. It is not fair to date a letter when you begin writing it, say on 7 January, eventually finish it on 9 January, keep it in your pocket until you have bought a stamp on 11 January, send it second class and then expect a response within seven days of the date of your letter. Use first-class post and, if you are concerned about safe receipt of the letter, send it by recorded delivery.

Keep a note in your diary of when the period you have specified within your letter will expire and allowing, say, two days more, immediately get ready to sue. There is no need to wait to see if payment is made. You can begin thinking about how you will phrase your claim.

Summary — letter before action

- Date your letter and address it to a known individual.
- Keep your letter short.
- Set out the facts unemotionally and accurately.
- State what compensation or other method of recompense you require.
- Give a time limit and stick to it.
- Keep a note of when the time limit expires.

Making a claim in the small claims court

This section shows you how to go about bringing a legal action your-self, without assistance from solicitors. It concentrates on a small claim for compensation. Larger claims would be brought in the High Court, and complicated cases, including custody disputes and injunc-tions, are best handled by someone with experience of such matters. Industrial tribunals, which are used for employment disputes, are addressed in Chapter 14.

You will be able to obtain free leaflets from your local county court giving advice on how to bring a small claim. Marshal all your informa-tion into a logical order, consider and discuss with friends the likely chances of success of your case, and if you decide to go ahead take multiple copies of relevant correspondence and then go along to the county court to issue a default summons and particulars of claim. The particulars set out the details of your claim. They may fit on the form requesting the issuing of a default summons, but if the form does not allow sufficient space separate particulars can be drawn up. The coun-ty court gives examples in their booklet on small claims, which you can use to help you.

The completion of this documentation should be typed up extremely carefully. For the most common types of claim the county court issues standard particulars of claim forms, which may be rele-vant to your circumstances.

The forms should be returned to the court with the fee, which varies depending on the nature of the claim. Court fees were substan-tially increased in 1997. Where no limit on the damages is claimed then the issue fee of £500 is payable to the court when a summons or writ is issued. There is a sliding scale. For claims under £10,000 the fee is £120. There are some exceptions in cases of financial hardship. Contact your local court for guidance.

The court then confirms that proceedings have been issued and if the defendant does nothing further when 14 days have expired, you can have 'judgment' entered against him or her. No fee is payable for such judgment, but the onus is on you to apply for judgment, so keep a careful note of when the time period expires.

The defendant may agree to the claim and offer a proposal for pay-ing the sum due or the defendant may dispute the claim. Where a defence is submitted by the defendant the date will be set down for an initial hearing. Where the claim is £3000 or less there will be an automatic reference to 'arbitration', ie a formalised discussion aimed at resolving the dispute, though either party may refuse to allow the matter to be arbitrated in this way. It is usually preferable with small claims to opt for arbitration. The proceedings are much less formal and legalistic and take place in what is known as the 'small claims court'.

The next stage, assuming that settlement of the dispute has not then occurred, will be 'discovery', when each party is obliged to disclose to the other the documents on which it is relying in the case. This is followed by an inspection of those documents by each side. You will then exchange statements from your witnesses. At the trial or arbitration hearing you will be required to describe your case and may call witnesses on your behalf. Practise beforehand what you will say.

Where you win at the trial or on arbitration, or you obtain judgment as the defendant fails to defend the proceedings or admits liability, you will then need to have the judgment enforced against the defendant, as mentioned in Chapter 4.

Defending yourself

Where the position is reversed, and you are being sued, again there is no legal obligation to use solicitors, unless the defendant is a limited company, although you may feel happier doing so and you may be eligible for Legal Aid. Civil proceedings in the county court will follow the form described in the previous section. It is important to ensure that you defend the proceedings by returning the court form in time, and that you similarly take time and effort to prepare your defence to the action.

Summary — do-it-yourself legal action

- Do-it-yourself legal proceedings are always possible.
- They are best used for simple cases such as a debt owed or for proceeding against a supplier of faulty goods.
- Small claims should be brought in the county court.
- Prepare your case well and obtain as much assistance from the court as possible.
- Stick to time limits.

6
Buying a House

Buying a house or flat is often the only time when many people come into contact with solicitors and the law. Although it is possible to do the legal work, known as 'conveyancing', yourself, it is not advisable. In the present economic climate many solicitors are offering very good conveyancing deals of a few hundred pounds only, for what can be a very complicated job. The best way to proceed is to shop around for 'quotes' from a number of different solicitors' firms, preferably choosing a firm which someone you know has used, where they were happy with the service which was offered. There are books available on how to do your own conveyancing, but the time, effort and worry involved is not justified. The solicitors' fees will be a small proportion of the overall costs of the transaction, which will also include:

- stamp duty (1 per cent of the whole purchase price on purchases over £60,000; 1.5 per cent from £250,000 to £500,000; and 2 per cent for properties over £500,000);
- search fees;
- Land Registry fees;
- survey/valuation fees;
- estate agents' fees, where you are also selling a property and have not chosen to advertise it yourself;
- mortgage arrangement fee may be payable for special mortgage deals;
- mortgage indemnity premium, where you are borrowing a large percentage of the purchase price.

There are also all the usual costs of moving home, such as removal firms and essential repairs to the property.

This chapter gives an overview of the conveyancing system and describes what your solicitor does for his or her money. It does not show how you can do conveyancing yourself, but should give some insight into the process of buying a house.

'Conveyancing' is simply the process of buying a house or flat. The reason the process can be complicated and time-consuming is because large sums of money are at stake. Most of the searches and checks which the solicitor undertakes are to ensure that the purchaser is buying what he or she thinks they are buying, and to ensure that the property is owned by the purchaser and not subject to the rights of third parties.

At the end of this chapter you will find a chart which shows the typical steps in a conveyancing transaction.

It is important to note at this stage that the conveyancing process is different in Scotland.

Making an offer

The first stage of the conveyancing process is finding a property to buy. Most people are aware that they are not legally bound to buy a property until they have exchanged contracts with the seller or 'vendor'. Having viewed a number of properties the purchaser usually contacts the estate agent handling the sale of the preferred property and makes an offer to purchase. The offer should be expressed to be 'subject to contract'. This means that the offer is not legally binding on the purchaser, who may change the amount offered subsequently, particularly if a survey shows that the property is in fact worth considerably less than the offer.

The initial offer may be for the asking price or less and negotiation may then take place over the price. Raise at this stage the question of purchase of carpets and curtains, and any other items not otherwise included in the sale, or later on you can be asked to pay extra for such items or move in and find that all the light fittings have been removed.

Speed and timing

When an offer is made, the estate agent will ask for details of your solicitor, so obtain quotes and choose a firm as soon as possible. The process of purchasing a house frequently takes up to three months and sometimes longer, particularly where there are a number of sellers and purchasers in a 'chain' all aiming to sell and purchase on the same day. Even where there is a cash or first-time buyer and a seller with nowhere else to buy, the process is likely to take months in most cases. However, conveyancing *can* be achieved within days in cases of extreme urgency, where the finance is readily available and all parties pull out all the stops to achieve a speedy completion.

Offers are not binding under English law. Until contracts are exchanged either party can pull out of the transaction without any obligation to the other party.

This means that you could lose your survey and solicitors' and search fees expended in a transaction which proves abortive. There is little that can be done to mitigate this problem. If you buy a property at auction this means that once an offer is made the purchaser must proceed, but again the cost of a survey must be incurred before the auction and before the purchaser knows whether or not he or she will succeed in their bid.

Instructing a solicitor

Your solicitor will need to know from you:

- who is buying and selling the property – full names and addresses;
- which solicitors are acting for the other party;
- details of your mortgage, if you will be obtaining one;
- the purchase price and what it includes;
- the address of the property and a copy of the estate agent's particulars.

If you treat every communication as being urgent then the transaction is likely to proceed more quickly. Reply to letters as a matter of priority, deliver letters/mortgage application forms by hand where possible, telephone all parties frequently for progress reports, communicate clearly and find out the real reasons for any delays.

Before exchange of contracts

Before the parties exchange contracts they are free to withdraw at any stage. In that period you will have a survey or valuation carried out. It is always safer to have a full structural survey, since although this may not be a requirement for your mortgage, it protects you. A building society valuation will not be anything like as thorough as a full structural survey of the building.

Your solicitor will obtain a local search, either from the seller or the relevant authorities. This search, for which you are required to pay, is produced by the local authority and informs the purchaser of issues such as whether the property is connected to the public sewerage system, and whether the street is adopted by the local authority or privately owned. The local search does not reveal what planning applications might have been put in by neighbours, though, so it is always worth going to the local planning office yourself to check on this.

If you are selling, the sale can be speeded up by your solicitor obtaining the search to pass on to the buyer. Ask your solicitor to arrange this. Indeed, your solicitor will automatically do so if he or she follows the Law Society's Protocol scheme. You may obtain a swifter service if your solicitor does follow this scheme, so check before instructing anyone.

The seller will be required to answer a long series of questions about the property, dealing with many relevant issues, such as whether planning permission was obtained for various extensions to the premises, whether the property has been treated for woodworm or dry rot and if there are guarantees for this work which can be passed on to the purchaser. Ask your solicitor to send you a copy of the response. This can be very interesting and can tell you more about the property, although the solicitor is also likely to summarise, in a 'report on title', the salient points later on for your benefit.

The seller prepares a draft contract, which is likely to comprise a standard form contract produced by the Law Society. The draft contract will then be approved or amended by the purchaser.

Freehold and leasehold

Houses are generally sold freehold, ie the purchaser buys the property for ever and can pass it down through succeeding generations of their family. Most flats, however, are sold on long leases, not short-term tenancies as for rented property, but leases of 90-plus years. When the lease expires the property reverts to the 'freeholder'.

Some flat owners have purchased their own freehold, which may be owned by a separate company. The Leasehold Reform, Housing and Urban Development Act 1993 came into force on 1 November 1993. This gives some leaseholders rights to purchase their freehold or extend their lease where two-thirds of leaseholders in a block agree. Compensation to the freeholder for such expropriation, known as the 'marriage value', must be paid. This is likely to amount to several thousand pounds for the average lease on a flat. When buying a leasehold property bear in mind that leases under about 40 years are difficult to raise a mortgage on and may be hard to sell. Longer leases are not a problem, but ask other flat owners about their experiences of dealing with the freeholder, what service charges there are, and how promptly repairs and insurance claims are handled.

Where the property is leasehold then the solicitor will need to check carefully the terms of the lease which the purchaser will have to accept on completion of the transaction. It is worth the purchaser reading the lease, for it is likely to contain a number of obligations and restrictions in relation to the property.

Registered and unregistered land

Most properties purchased are on what is known as 'registered land', for which a Land Certificate is available, proving the seller's ownership of the property. Gradually, the whole country is being officially registered in this way, but it is taking some time due to the scale of the task. Where the title is unregistered there will be no Land Certificate, so the solicitor will have to enquire and check carefully into the history of ownership of the land.

The solicitor for the purchaser will, thus, receive the local search, replies to enquiries about the property, a draft contract, lease (where the property is leasehold) and Land Certificate (where the property is on registered land). When this documentation has been checked on your behalf and a mortgage offer obtained, the parties can then proceed to exchange of contracts.

Exchange of contracts

There is a two-stage process in conveyancing. The purchaser does not own the property until the contract is 'completed', which is a period after exchange of contracts. A typical period between exchange and completion is two weeks to a month.

The purchaser then reads the contract carefully, checking details of the names of the parties, and the purchase price and what it includes, and then returns it to the seller with the deposit. Usually 10 per cent of the purchase price is put up at this stage, though that is not compulsory. The deposit is forfeited if the parties exchange contracts and then the purchaser does not proceed to complete the purchase, so purchasers prefer a deposit of 10 per cent. However, where the purchaser is borrowing 95 per cent of the purchase price, it may be possible to negotiate that only 5 per cent is paid on exchange of contracts.

The contract will set out the completion date – this is the date when the purchaser moves into the property. It may be possible to negotiate a right to enter a vacant property before completion to carry out repairs or other works to the premises. This should be agreed before exchange of contracts. Even though the purchaser does not own the property after exchange of contracts, the purchaser is required to effect insurance of the property at this point. The bank or building society from whom the loan is obtained will usually arrange this.

After exchange

After exchange of contracts the solicitor for the purchaser carries out an official search at the Land Registry and sends a series of questions to the seller about his or her title to the land. A draft transfer deed is then prepared. This is the legal document, subject to stamp duty, which formally completes the sale transaction, as initially agreed in the contract.

Your solicitor draws up a completion statement, setting out what money will be due on completion. Check this carefully. Given the 'large volume, low charge' conveyancing transactions which some solicitors carry out it is not surprising that mistakes can be made. Final checks then take place on whether the seller is bankrupt and as to whether there have been any recent changes in the seller's ownership of the land.

Completion

The final stage is 'completion', when the purchaser takes over the property and receives the keys. The solicitor attends to the payment of stamp duty and the new owner is registered at the Land Registry as the owner of the property.

The chart below summarises the legal procedures. Your solicitor should explain these stages to you throughout the transaction.

Steps in a conveyancing transaction

- Buyer makes offer on property.
- Mortgage application submitted and survey done.
- Solicitors instructed by the parties.
- Local search obtained and enquiries answered concerning the property.
- Lease, Land Registry certificate and contract examined by the purchaser's solicitor.
- Once mortgage offer through and survey contracts exchanged — purchaser pays 10 per cent deposit.

BOTH PARTIES NOW MUST GO AHEAD

- Property insured by buyer.
- Purchaser's solicitor inspects title at Land Registry and sends questions concerning title to seller.
- Draft transfer deed prepared, final searches.
- Completion statement prepared showing what sums will be due from purchaser on completion.
- Completion of the transaction. Move in.

THE HOUSE IS NOW YOURS.

- Purchaser's solicitor pays stamp duty and registers the purchaser as legal owner of the property. Unless there is no mortgage, the lender retains the title deeds.

To finish this chapter, it is appropriate to mention that many, many house buying transactions fall through for a number of reasons, some legal. These include:

- a survey revealing substantial problems of damp, woodworm, subsidence, etc;
- the purchaser or seller simply changing their mind, or their purchaser or seller pulling out, so disrupting the chain;
- the purchaser being refused a mortgage;
- defects in the title to the property or disputes over ownership.

Be prepared to accept inevitable set-backs. The next property you find could well, in the end, prove a better buy.

7
Getting into debt

This chapter considers the legal consequences of getting into debt and, in particular, bankruptcy. Credit is widely available and advertising rarely emphasises the burden of repayment of loans. It hardly needs saying that if money is borrowed it must be repaid. Loans should never be approached frivolously and repayment should be regarded as a serious business. Failure to pay a debt, however small, can lead to bankruptcy and credit blacklisting. When your financial situation improves it may be impossible to take out a mortgage or obtain a small bank loan because of past debts.

The best position is never to have failed to pay debts in the first place, so every effort should be put into repaying and reducing them.

Agencies which can help

There are a number of voluntary agencies available to help those people finding themselves in financial difficulties, including the Citizens' Advice Bureaux, and church and voluntary organisations.

These agencies will help you draw up a list of your current income and outgoings, and help you to prioritise payments according to the consequences of non-payment of items such as the rent/mortgage, water rates, council tax, heating and telephone bills, credit and store card debts, and other expenses. There is no reason why you cannot undertake this exercise yourself, drawing up a list with columns of all your outgoings and income.

Insurance

By careful budgeting and a cautious approach to the taking out of loans the risk of getting into debt can be reduced. However, for many people unforeseen circumstances, in particular redundancy and illness, mean that getting into financial difficulties cannot be avoided. It is possible to take out insurance in advance against many of the circumstances which lead people into debt including the following.

- There is a form of life insurance, called term assurance, which only pays out on death. It is quite cheap.
- Permanent health insurance provides cover against long-term sickness, rendering the insured unable to work through sickness. There are also more particular forms of such insurance which can be taken out, for example, to cover the cost of nursing care for the aged or to provide cover against certain dread diseases. Private health insurance, which gives the insured choice over when, for example, an operation is carried out, can reduce financial loss, in so far as a self-employed person can arrange a hospital appointment or operation around the needs of their business.
- Many building societies and banks now require borrowers to take out insurance with them in the form of mortgage protection policies to ensure that the mortgage is paid in the event of redundancy.
- Many credit card and store card companies offer optional insurance cover against redundancy.
- Various policies are available to cover the cost of a funeral and burial/cremation.
- Legal expenses insurance is available to cover the cost of legal fees in various circumstances.

Always check that your employer does not already provide cover for any or all of these circumstances and obtain advice from an independent financial adviser. For example, only those with dependants are likely to need life insurance.

Enforcement of judgments

Where a debt is not paid when due and the creditor has gone to court over the matter, then a judgment against you will be recorded. The creditor then has the judgment enforced against you. If you have not sent them a valid cheque or paid in cash the money due, then there are a variety of ways of enforcing the debt against you.

It is possible to get an attachment of earnings order, which allows the creditor to have the sum due, usually in regular instalments, deducted from your salary before your employer hands it over to you. Other methods include a charging order over any property which you own. This means that you could lose the property if you fail to pay the debt. Of course, some loans, notably mortgages for the purchase of a home, are 'secured' by a charge over your property already. You could, therefore, lose your home if you fail to pay the debt. Some personal loans advertised at attractive interest rates are able to offer competitive rates, because hidden among the small print is a requirement that you take out a second mortgage over your home.

The creditor can also send in the bailiffs to levy execution. Bailiffs are not allowed to break into premises, but they can enter through unlocked windows and doors. Once inside they will take goods which, when sold, will be sufficient to pay the debt due. The goods which they may take must belong to the debtor and can include money, but they may not seize:

- goods necessary for the debtor to carry out his or her job, such as tools, books, vans, etc;
- goods necessary to fulfil the basic needs of the debtor, such as food, beds and clothes. Televisions, videos, stereos etc, however, are not regarded as essential.

Goods which are owned by another person, such as the wife or husband of the debtor, or goods owned by a shop or credit company being bought on credit, cannot be seized.

Bankruptcy and liquidation

A more drastic step which a creditor can take against a debtor is to have the debtor declared bankrupt. 'Bankruptcy' is the term used for individuals, while 'liquidation' is used for companies. If you run a business it is important to distinguish to whom debts are owed. If you operate through a limited company then any debts will be those of the company and you will not be liable. However, many banks, in granting loans to small companies, require the owners to give personal guarantees or charges over their own homes, so the advantage of operating through a limited liability company is lost for those debts. Other debts, though, may only be those of the company.

Those operating through a partnership or trading as individual sole traders, but using another business name, will be personally liable for all the debts of the business.

It is wise to consider liquidation, administration (where a breathing space from creditors is granted to companies to put their affairs in order) and bankruptcy with someone legally qualified, particularly for companies. For individuals, bankruptcy may be instigated by a creditor or an individual may choose to go bankrupt themselves. A person may decide that the level of their debts has reached such a point that bankruptcy is the only option, so they may as well initiate the procedure before one of their creditors does.

Always consider whether it is possible to enter into voluntary arrangements with creditors before becoming bankrupt. If you are open with all creditors about your financial situation and offer to pay back debts at a certain rate over a stated period, then the creditors may accept such arrangement and you may avoid bankruptcy. On bankruptcy all the assets of the bankrupt are vested in the trustee in bankruptcy. There is no return of the assets on discharge of the bankruptcy, ie when the bankruptcy is over. A court order is needed to evict a bankrupt where children under 18 live in the family home.

If you begin the bankruptcy proceedings yourself then discharge (or freedom) from bankruptcy comes after two years in simple cases. Otherwise the period is three years. When the period expires an application should be made for a certificate of discharge. Anyone who has been bankrupt twice in the previous 15 years must apply for a discharge by order of the court. Once discharge is achieved there is generally no obligation to pay the previous debts.

The consequences of bankruptcy

Although for most people being forbidden from becoming an MP would not be a serious blow and the prospect of shaking off debts may appear to be the answer to all their problems, there are serious consequences of becoming bankrupt, which should be considered carefully before any decision is reached. Below is a summary of the main consequences of personal bankruptcy.

The consequences of personal bankruptcy

- All assets except 'necessaries' are handed over to the trustee in bankruptcy, ie lose all possessions, houses, shares etc.
- Bankruptcy must be disclosed before obtaining credit. This means credit is unlikely to be available.
- The bankruptcy and undischarged judgment debts will become known to potential creditors and credit rating and reference agencies used by most companies, banks etc. **The bankrupt will appear on a credit blacklist.**
- Without access to credit it is hard to start a new business — any old business will vest in the trustee in bankruptcy, along with the other assets.
- Any new business must be run under the bankrupt's full name, so credit checking can be carried out.
- Before discharge, a bankrupt cannot be a company director, so cannot run a business through a company.
- Bankrupts cannot be MPs, general medical practitioners, local councillors, solicitors or barristers until the bankruptcy is discharged.

8
Marriage and children

This chapter looks at the legal side of getting married and having children. The next chapter considers divorce. Although many couples choose not to marry and simply live together, the law does not treat married and unmarried couples in the same way. Chapter 16 deals with wills and deaths, and considers the differences in inheritance law between the married and unmarried.

Requirements for marriage

No one can be forced to marry. Marriage must be voluntary and the couple must both be 16 years or older and unmarried. Under the age of 18 the consent of the couple's parents is necessary. However, a marriage without such consent will still be valid, although a criminal offence will have been committed. Marriages between people of 15 and under will not be valid, nor will marriages between members of the same sex, even after a sex-change operation. Also, there are laws forbidding marriage between close relatives, such as between a man and his aunt, niece, mother-in-law or stepdaughter. Marriages between first cousins are allowed.

Getting married

Marriages are either according to the rites of the Church of England or through a civil ceremony (which may be incorporated into a marriage according to the rites of some other Christian denomination or other religion). Both methods require certain formalities to be followed. In the Church of England either the banns are read in the couple's parish churches (ie an announcement of the impending marriage is made) or a licence is obtained. For other marriages a registrar's certificate is required. Marriages can now be formalised anywhere which is licensed, including hotels and stately homes.

This book deals with English law. Marriages abroad are conducted according to the laws of other lands, in some cases in countries where polygamous marriages and marriages to those under 16 are permitted. English law will recognise such marriages, though detailed advice should be sought for difficult cases. Marriages will also be conducted in the UK according to the canon, or religious, law of particular faiths. These laws, particularly on subjects such as the remarriage of divorced people, will not always coincide with the civil marriage rules considered here.

The consequences of marriage

Marriage gives a couple the right to a share of the property and other assets of the other person. They will also benefit for tax purposes from the married couple's tax allowance. Women do not have to change their name or use the designation 'Mrs', though many do. Marriage implies consent to sexual intercourse on a 'reasonable' basis, though a husband can now be convicted of the rape of his wife.

It is possible to draw up a marriage contract before or during marriage, which deals with the division of assets in the event of a break-up of the marriage. This is known as a pre-nuptial agreement. However, the legal effectiveness of such contracts is doubtful.

Registration of the birth of children

The first legal formality in connection with the birth of children is to register their birth within six weeks. The father's name will be registered when the couple are married. When they are unmarried and the father wants his name to appear, and the mother agrees, then his name will be registered. Where the father does not consent, the mother must obtain a court order. The child can be given any first names. The surname can be that of the mother or a joint surname of mother and father. A short-form birth certificate is issued free. It can be wise to order three or more extra certificates at birth as these are always useful later and do not cost very much.

Adopting and fostering

Those wishing to adopt a child in England and Wales should apply to their local social services department for a list of adoption agencies.

An adopted child receives a new birth certificate which does not reveal its original parents' names, but at the age of 18 an adopted child has the right to trace details of its true parents, though there is no such right for the parents. An Adoption Contact Register is kept by the Registrar of Births, Marriages and Deaths, where both parents and children can register their details.

There is a general shortage of new babies for adoption in the UK and some parents go abroad to find a suitable child. Although surrogate motherhood is not against the law, the paying of money for another woman to have a child for you is, except for payment of her expenses. Techniques now make it possible for the genetic child of a couple to be gestated within the womb of a host mother; a stranger or relative. Adoption is necessary after the child is born in such circumstances. Anyone contemplating such arrangements should take legal advice as to the relative rights and obligations of the genetic and host parents, and draw up an agreement addressing the issues of medical expenses, the child being born with disabilities and either side changing their mind. The host mother may have the right to change her mind about keeping the child afterwards.

Fostered children are those looked after by foster-parents for, generally, shorter periods. Some fostering is long term and the natural parents are simply not prepared to sign the necessary adoption papers.

Children and their care

The obligations of parenthood include the care and control of their children. Parents may use a reasonable amount of force in disciplining their children and may consent to physical punishment of their children by others, though physical punishment is no longer allowed in State schools.

Difficulties with custody of children arise on divorce, when residency orders may need to be agreed under the Children Act 1989. For more information on divorce and children, see Chapter 9.

Where the parents are unmarried the mother has the sole legal rights and responsibilities for any children. Where the father wants his say in the upbringing of the children then he must reach agreement with the mother or go to court. The mother will still be able to obtain maintenance from the father for the support of the child.

DNA testing of cell structures with 100 per cent accuracy is now available to prove or disprove parenthood. Cheaper blood tests are not quite as reliable. Fathers cannot be forced to undertake a test, but have the right to apply for a legal responsibility order and ask the court to carry out a DNA test. The Child Support Agency traces and enforces maintenance awards against missing parents. For more on this see Chapter 9.

Since the Children Act 1989 came into force in 1991, children now have the right to apply to the court to 'divorce' themselves from their parents or to oblige one parent in a broken marriage to visit them.

Legal issues of child care

Increasingly, children under five are supported by two working parents. Weekday care of the child is given to relatives, friends, childminders, nurseries, nursery schools, playgroups and nannies or a mixture of these. Nurseries, nursery schools and childminders are required to be registered by the local authority, and are subject to inspections and requirements concerning the ratio of adult carers to the number of children under particular ages. A carer looking after your children in your own home, such as a nanny does not currently have to register.

In all cases it is wise to draw up a short agreement setting out what has been agreed and any special requirements for the children, such as religious or other dietary rules, how they should be disciplined etc.

The wages of domestic employees should be paid under the PAYE (pay as you earn) system, a simplified domestic scheme for which information is available from the Inland Revenue. Payment of such tax ensures that the carer has a National Insurance contribution record, state sickness and maternity benefits etc. Failure to pay tax on employees' wages can lead to fines and even jail sentences.

Education

Parents have an obligation to see that their children are educated. Most send their children to the local State school. However, parents have the right to educate their children themselves at home, or to employ a tutor, or to send their child to a private, secular or religious day or boarding school. Church of England, Catholic and Jewish voluntary schools are also available, although to date no such status has been granted to a Muslim school. All State and independent schools, and parents educating their children at home, are subject to inspection by the authorities.

Parents can choose to send their children to State schools either locally or in a different education authority area. However, schools often operate selection criteria based on where children live. Church schools have criteria based on baptism, church attendance and involvement in parish life, as well as similar criteria to that of other State schools, such as where you live and whether siblings are at the school. Popular schools are often over-subscribed and although appeals are possible, there can be no guarantee that a child will obtain a place at the parents' first choice of school.

Parents should choose schools, consider prospectuses and examination results, and register their children at schools as soon as possible. Many parents move house to be near their preferred school and may have children tutored for academically selective schools (usually in the private sector).

State schools are obliged to follow the National Curriculum which requires compulsory subjects to be taught in schools and that children are regularly tested. This was brought in by the Education Reform Act of 1988. Although schools are recommended to do so, there is no legal obligation to provide parents with an annual school report on their child.

Schools have the right to suspend, exclude and expel children from school for disruptive behaviour. However, where a child is expelled, the local education authority has an obligation to provide education for the child, either at another school or with a tutor. Parents should ascertain in advance what the policy of a particular school is on subjects such as uniform, standards of dress, religious dietary requirements, sex education and any other contentious issues before choosing the school for their child to avoid problems later. Persistent truanting and misbehaviour can result in the child, ultimately, being taken into the care of the local authority.

Children and crime

Where a young person is taken to court and ordered to pay fines, the parents must pay up unless it would be 'unreasonable' for them to do so. Children under the age of ten cannot be convicted of a criminal offence. However, a persistent offender under ten could be taken into local authority care. Children of ten and over can be convicted where it can be shown that they knew what they were doing was wrong. Once 14 or over, a boy can be convicted of rape.

Summary — marriage and children

- Further details of the legal formalities of marriage and registration of births can be obtained from your local town hall or civic centre.
- Legal advice on the legal issues of childcare, the responsibilities of absent fathers or mothers and schooling can be obtained from solicitors, law centres or Citizens' Advice Bureaux.
- Local authorities and local education authorities can advise on registration of nurseries and childminders, and issues concerning schooling.

9
Divorce

This chapter describes the basic steps necessary to divorce. Divorce is not the only solution to marital breakdown. Various forms of separation are possible, which do not go as far as a divorce and, in rare cases, such as non-consummation of the marriage, the marriage may be annulled, which would allow the couple to remarry in church (otherwise a church wedding is not usually possible for divorced people, though a church blessing is possible in the Church of England).

This chapter first sets out the current divorce law. The Family Law Act 1996 will not be fully in force until 1999 and will alter much of which is written here. The second part of this chapter provides an overview of the Act.

The ground for divorce

There is only one ground for divorce – that the marriage has irretrievably broken down. However, that is proven by one of five different factors:

- adultery;
- two years' separation, with consent of the other party;
- desertion for at least two years;
- five years' separation, without consent.

However, no divorce is permitted unless the marriage has lasted at least one year.

Divorce is one legal area when it is best to approach a solicitor. Legal Aid will be available for those within its narrow financial limits, see page 17, but not where the divorce is undefended.

Adultery

It must be shown that the other party has committed adultery (ie had sexual intercourse with another person) and the spouse petitioning for divorce finds it intolerable to live with them. Enquiry agents are often engaged by one spouse to determine whether or not adultery is taking place. Provided the petitioning spouse does not live with their husband or wife for more than six months after they discover the adultery, the 'tolerance' shown by living together for up to six months will not prevent the use of the adultery to prove that the marriage has irretrievably broken down. The third party involved in the adultery will be named in the divorce petition.

You cannot rely on your own adultery to obtain a divorce.

Unreasonable behaviour

'Unreasonable behaviour' is the most commonly used reason for divorce and covers a multitude of different circumstances. Indeed it has been argued that anyone, even in a happy marriage, could dredge up sufficient facts to found a case for unreasonable behaviour. However, there are cases where unreasonable behaviour cannot be shown. It is necessary to decide whether any ordinary person would regard it as reasonable in all the circumstances for the petitioner to continue to live with their spouse.

Violence, drunkenness, obsessive behaviour, refusal to have sexual intercourse or children, and bad nagging could all amount to unreasonable behaviour. Medical evidence and the evidence of neighbours, relatives and friends can be crucial in proving unreasonable behaviour. Living together for up to six months after the act of unreasonable behaviour is possible without jeopardising the case.

Two years' separation with consent

Where the couple have lived apart for two years, and both agree, then they can divorce. However, if the other party objects and there is no unreasonable behaviour or adultery then a period of five years must elapse before divorce is possible. Many couples use the two years' separation situation to achieve an amicable divorce. It removes the need to draw up lists of unreasonable behaviour or show adultery, which involves naming the third party involved.

Even where a couple share a house it may be possible to show separation, provided they maintain separate lives in the same house. The couple may live together for up to six months during the period of 'separation', attempting a reconciliation without jeopardising the two-year separation period for divorce.

Desertion for two years

This ground is rarely used and requires that the couple have lived apart for at least two years, one has voluntarily deserted the other and the other does not agree to the separation, and finally, the desertion must have been without justifiable cause.

Living apart for five years

Where there is no unreasonable behaviour or adultery and one spouse does not consent to a divorce, all the other party to the marriage can do is to wait five years. A temporary (up to six months) period of reconciliation (ie living together) is permitted during this five-year period.

There is a defence which can be used by the party opposing the divorce in these circumstances that the divorce would cause **grave financial or other hardship and that it would be wrong in all the circumstances to grant the divorce**. This special defence is rarely allowed by the courts, however.

Reconciliation

All couples should attempt reconciliation before going to a solicitor for a divorce. Many families are thrown into poverty by divorce, children suffer and second marriages have a high failure rate. Many agencies offer free advice, including Relate (previously known as the Marriage Guidance Council) and clergymen, family therapists etc may all have a role to play if one or other partner wishes to get outside help.

Instructing a solicitor

However, when every avenue has been explored and reconciliation is impossible, the first stage is to see a solicitor. The solicitor's fees will be reduced where his or her work is minimised. Supplying all relevant information in advance, therefore, can reduce fees. Details of the couple and children, and their names and addresses, as well as their financial circumstances, should be prepared in advance in writing. Few divorces cost under £1000, so assisting the solicitor to a speedy resolution of the matter will help keep costs low.

Divorce procedure

Where the divorce is undefended, ie the other party does not contest it, then there is no court appearance when the divorce petition is lodged, unless there are other disputes such as over any children or financial arrangements. Most disputes are over children and money, and not over the divorce itself. A copy of your marriage certificate is required, and you or your solicitor needs to complete a divorce petition and a statement of arrangements for the children, and pay the court fee, when lodging the petition.

The court deals with sending the petition to the other spouse, who is required to return an acknowledgement of service form, which is then forwarded by the court to the party seeking the divorce, known as the 'petitioner'. It is on this acknowledgement that the other party will indicate whether or not they propose to defend the divorce. The court also sends the petitioner a form of 'affidavit' or statement to be sworn, setting out the facts of the divorce petition with any evidence which is available. A directions for trial form should also be completed.

The affidavit will need to be sworn by you in front of a solicitor. The current fee (1997) is £5 for the affidavit and £2 for each exhibit (or evidence) attached.

All the papers go to a district judge, who determines whether or not a divorce should be granted and may set a date for the 'decree nisi', ie the first decision. Where the judge deems it necessary, a formal court order concerning the children may be ordered, and welfare reports and a court hearing arranged.

There is no need to attend court for the decree nisi. A period of six weeks will expire between the decree nisi and the decree absolute (when the divorce becomes final). Only after the decree absolute are the parties to the marriage free to marry again. Marriage before that date will be bigamous, void and a crime. It is necessary to apply for a decree absolute and the solicitor for the petitioner will advise on this.

Divorces usually take under six months to finalise, but can become acrimonious where there is dispute over with which parent the children should live or over money – maintenance or division of assets.

Money

On divorce the richer spouse is generally obliged to help support the poorer spouse financially. This usually means that husbands support wives, though maintenance payments by wife to husband are ordered where the wife has the greater earnings. Obligations to maintain children are dealt with entirely separately. The parent without custody will also have to honour their financial obligations to their children.

In 1993 the Child Support Act 1991 came into force. This states that the Child Support Agency must be used by parents on welfare benefits to calculate and enforce maintenance for their children from the other parent. The parent with whom the child resides will not necessarily be the mother, though in practice it often is. The Child Support Agency traces the missing parent and enforces maintenance orders against them, which can be made by direct deduction from the wages of the ex-spouse.

In many cases a 'clean break' between husband and wife may be agreed, particularly where there are no children and the marriage has been short. This means a settlement is reached, with one ex-spouse paying the other off, once and for all, with no future obligation to maintain the other party. However, the Child Support Agency has effectively overturned some clean break orders, putting the clean break principle into doubt.

Long-term maintenance by one spouse to the other is often agreed. As a very general rule, the income of both spouses is added together and the spouse with the lower income receives a third of the total. However, much will depend on the individual circumstances. The very rich may simply have to pay a sum sufficient to ensure the other partner's lifestyle may continue as before. It is wise to seek legal advice before agreeing to any arrangements concerning the future financial situation after a divorce.

The Child Support Agency has to apply rigid criteria in determining how much maintenance one ex-spouse should pay to the other, which, to date, does not always reflect earlier court orders, such as the transfer of assets on divorce to achieve a clean break. These difficulties are likely to be sorted out through court action or legislation.

The term 'custody' is no longer used in relation to arrangements for the care of children. Since the Children Act 1989 came into force in 1991 the relevant term used is 'parental responsibility'. The divorce will not be made absolute until arrangements for the children have been finalised. Under the Children Act parents can reach their own agreement over the care of their children. It is only if they cannot reach agreement that the court will be forced to make an order. The parties will then become involved in expensive court proceedings which are best avoided if at all possible.

The Family Law Act 1996

The Family Law Act 1996 at the date of writing (September 1997) is not yet in force. However it will radically change divorce law. It is likely to be fully in force by 1999 and therefore is described in outline below. All family law solicitors can advise you on the Act and its implications. The Act not only changes the law on divorce but also the law on domestic violence. The stages in a divorce will be as follows:

Information meeting

At least three months before a divorce is applied for the person wanting the divorce must attend a Divorce Information Meeting. The other spouse must attend the same or a separate meeting if there are children or financial matters to sort out. An information pack will be handed out and the parties encouraged to attend marriage guidance.

Statement of marital breakdown

The next stage is that one spouse files a statement of marital breakdown simply saying the marriage has broken down. There is no statement of adultery, unreasonable behaviour or any other grounds. No such statement can be filed until at least one year after the marriage, whether the statement is in relation to a divorce or a judicial separation. So no one can apply for divorce until they have been married for at least one year.

Reflection and consideration period and future arrangements

There then follows a period for reflection and consideration – a period of nine months during which arrangements for the future of the parties are made. The nine month period can be extended another six months (to a total of 15 months) if there is a child involved, on application by the spouse who has not applied for the divorce. The arrangements for the future in relation to children and financial matters must be approved by the court *before* the divorce can go ahead. In certain cases the parties can be forced to attend a mediation session.

Divorce order

The court will then make the divorce or separation order when it is satisfied that the requirements above have been met. There is a new hardship bar which can enable one spouse to prevent a divorce going ahead at all. This might apply for example, to religious reasons or on grounds related to a child of the family. The Act also changes some of the terms used in divorce: the words decree nisi and decree absolute are abolished for example.

Finally always seek up to date legal advice in this field. For example changes in the rules in relation to rights to splitting of a spouse's pension are expected in the next few years and this is in general a fast moving legal field at present.

Summary — divorce

- Determine if the marriage has lasted over one year and has irretrievably broken down by applying one of the five circumstances described previously.
- Try reconciliation, perhaps using an outside mediator, Relate, a priest etc.
- Instruct a solicitor who will advise you of the procedure for a divorce.
- Agree as much as possible with your spouse to keep costs down and avoid acrimony, particularly where children are concerned. The Children Act 1989 gives greater flexibility for parents to reach their own agreement on parental responsibility.
- Consider financial arrangements and arrangements for the children early on. Obtain legal advice before agreeing.
- The Child Support Agency must be used by those on State benefits to enforce maintenance against an absent parent. Other parents have a choice as to whether or not to use the services of the agency.
- Note the Family Law Act 1996, when in force, will alter the law radically.

10
Getting paid

Many people are owed money, often in business, but sometimes also in their personal life. This chapter looks at practical ways to recover money owed and the legal remedies which are available to enforce a debt.

Reducing risk

Credit checks

Always check the creditworthiness of anyone to whom money is to be advanced. Credit reference agencies keep details of individuals against whom court judgment debts have been awarded, and enquiries of other companies, colleagues and contacts should enable some background information to be obtained before a loan is made.

Always write to the borrower's bank for a bank reference and also follow up other references which the borrower may offer as to their creditworthiness.

Secured loans

In some cases in business it may be possible to arrange a secured loan, where property is used as security of the loan. If the borrower defaults then the lender can sell the property. Such secured loans, charges or mortgages should be registered and legal advice should be sought.

Guarantees

In other cases, it is wise to make the owners of a company liable in addition to the company itself or require the company or individual to offer a bank or parent company guarantee of the loan.

Terms and conditions of business

Have clear terms and conditions of business put down in writing, which contain payment periods. It is usual to stipulate that payment is due within a certain number of days, for example 30, of the date of invoice and that interest will be charged at a fixed percentage over bank base rate from time to time for money which is overdue for payment. It is essential that the terms and conditions are made part of the contract between the parties, by drawing them to the attention of the other party before the contract is made. Including them on the back of the invoice, which will not be seen until after the goods have been sold or the work done, is not enough for them to be legally effective.

Retention of title clauses

In business, where goods are often sold on credit, consider including a 'retention' or 'reservation' of title clause in your standard conditions of sale. This clause states that although the buyer has purchased the goods and taken possession of them they remain your goods until payment has been made. Then, as long as the clause is properly drafted, if the buyer goes into liquidation before paying you, you can enter the buyer's premises to take possession of your goods, rather than ranking with the general creditors of the business, who may well receive nothing.

Keeping a close eye

Always keep a close eye on debts and as soon as payment is due remind the customer. Many companies employ a credit controller whose job it is to monitor debts. Also, information about the financial standing of particular customers can be ascertained from other contacts in your trade. Some companies form or join 'credit circles', where competitors meet to discuss the creditworthiness of mutual customers. Such meetings should not, however, become a forum for exchange of information on prices, jobs available or terms of trading, or the Office of Fair Trading may investigate.

It is often the case that companies will pay those creditors which make the most nuisance of themselves. Constant telephone calls reminding the company of the debt can result in their paying you just to stop the telephone calls coming. However, many individuals are in the difficult position of not wanting to annoy a customer too much, as this could result in no further work or contracts. Late payment is better than no payment at all. Often a friendly call to your opposite number at the other company, when payment is getting particularly slow, can result in a cheque being paid.

Refusing to do further work may not always result in payment unless the other company is dependent on you and cannot use other suppliers. Where the company appears to be in serious financial difficulties, a request for payment of at least some of the money owed could result in a part payment. That might be better than waiting to see how many pence in the pound all creditors obtain on a liquidation, but bear in mind that the directors of the insolvent company could incur personal liability for preferring one creditor over another, so there may be legal reasons why they cannot pay you first.

Debt collectors and factors

Many companies employ professional debt collection agencies to collect their debts for them. Another alternative is to 'sell' the debts to a factoring company. The debts are sold at less than their full value as all of them may not be recovered, and the factor makes his or her money by recovering as many of the debts as possible and pocketing the difference. Factoring of debts can be good for cash flow, but might put some customers off.

Threatening letters

Where all 'peaceful' means have been employed to no avail against a debtor, then consider a threatening letter – not threats with menaces, blackmail or anything of that sort, or you will find yourself in trouble with the police, but a final warning letter. This states that if the money owed is not paid within a certain number of days from the date of the letter then solicitors will be instructed to begin legal proceedings. You may prefer to get your solicitor to draft the warning letter as it could frighten the debtor into paying up more quickly. However, in either case, carry through any threat. Extending the time limit again will just make you look silly.

An example of a letter follows below:

Your address
Date

Their address
Their reference
[name an individual
call first if you are not sure to whom to write]

Dear Mr Bloggs

XYZ Carpet Fitters

I am writing to draw your attention to the fact that our invoices numbered 1234 and 1449 are now more than two months overdue for payment. As you should be aware, clause 6 of our terms and conditions of business which were supplied to you before we began undertaking business for you with our original letter of 1 January 1984, entitle us to charge interest on sums overdue. At current rates this is running at X%pa and now totals £...

We have had very favourable comments from you concerning the work which we did in relation to these invoices and we therefore cannot understand why the invoices have not been paid. We have written to remind you on two separate occasions and no payment has been forthcoming.

As we are keen to continue to work for your company and in particular to undertake the carpet-fitting work at the XXX hotel in a month's time, we look forward to receiving your cheque.

If we do not receive a cheque for £XXX within seven days of the date of this letter, ie by 6 September 1994, we shall have no alternative but to instruct our solicitors to begin legal proceedings for recovery of the sum due, plus damages, costs and interest.

Yours sincerely

John Smith

Chapters 3 and 5 showed how to issue proceedings, either using a solicitor or on your own. Where a letter such as this does not result in payment of the sum owed, proceedings should be issued in the county court for recovery of the money. Threatening a bankruptcy petition or to put a company into liquidation can be a very effective enforcement method and should always be considered.

Where the company goes into liquidation, ensure that you recover all your goods at its premises. Making sure that goods are named as yours and stored separately helps in recovery. However, where you are simply owed an unsecured debt you will rank with the general creditors and may receive very little of your money once the expenses of the liquidation, wages, tax and National Insurance, secured loans etc have been paid.

Summary — getting paid

- Try not to offer credit in order to avoid the problems in this chapter. Some businesses are able to operate on a cash in advance basis.
- Where credit is offered, undertake credit checks first.
- Obtain security or guarantees for loans, if possible.
- Ensure you have clear terms and conditions of business, stating when payment is due and containing retention of title clauses where goods are being sold.
- Keep a close check on what sums are overdue. Good administration pays off.
- Be a nuisance to the debtor.
- Accept payment by instalments, if necessary.
- Consider employing a credit controller, debt collector and/or factoring debts.
- Send a final warning letter and, if the money is not then forthcoming, begin legal proceedings.

11
Property points and disputes with neighbours

This chapter looks at the most common property problems, such as planning permission and disputes with neighbours. Property law is a vast legal subject, so this chapter can only highlight some major areas as they affect individuals. Chapter 6 looked at buying a house. People requiring legal advice in connection with tenancy agreements can consult the Citizens' Advice Bureau, law centres and solicitors.

Your property

An Englishman's home may be his castle, but he cannot convert it into one. Generally, ownership does give householders rights to decorate their property as they choose, unless it falls within certain categories of listed building or is subject to restrictive covenants, for example requiring all the front doors in an attractive crescent of houses to be the same colour.

However, more major works may require planning permission and building regulations consent before works can go ahead.

Working from home

What you use your home for may well be restricted. Tenants are highly likely to have restrictions in their tenancy agreements which make it clear that no business may be carried on at the property. Check tenancy agreements carefully and ensure that the permission of the landlord is obtained in advance. Owners of leasehold properties, such as flats on a 90-year lease, may also be subject to restrictions on carrying on a business at the property. Freeholders may be subject to restrictive covenants arranged when the house was built, which may restrict the owner from carrying on business. Although consent from landlords may be possible, or even variation of leases or restrictive covenants agreed, these will not always be easy to achieve. The best way to proceed is to check the lease, etc before taking over the property.

The other area to consider is that of planning permission. Using any part of a home for business purposes needs planning permission, although the council is unlikely to have problems, for example, with a telesales operator or a company director who chooses to undertake paperwork at home a few days a week. Where the trade or business is likely to disturb the neighbours or result, for example, in used cars littering the pavement, then it will not be long before a visit from the planning department will occur. It is much better to obtain permission first or find business premises.

For example, say you practise complementary medicine. You decide to see clients to offer homoeopathic treatments at your semi-detached three-bedroom home, seeing patients in your living room. You should obtain planning permission, but you are unlikely to come to the attention of the planning authorities. However, business booms, so you decide to use your house as an alternative therapy centre, with each room dedicated to a different form of treatment. In this case there has been a change of use of the premises and planning permission must be obtained in advance.

Those working from home should also ensure that their business tools, fax machines, wordprocessors etc have business insurance cover as domestic policies may well not cover them. For tax purposes part of the heating, lighting, telephone bills etc may be tax deductible. A proportion of any capital gain made on the sale of the property may be liable to capital gains tax in such circumstances, so take advice. You may have to pay business rates and commercial rates for telephone use and power.

Planning permission

The planning laws are strict and people extending their house without consent can be obliged to tear down their expensive extension. There is no point in building and taking a risk. Neighbours may keep a close eye on developments and inform the local planning authorities.

It always pays to check whether planning permission is needed before embarking on any project, including a new fence, swimming pool, or even greenhouse or garden shed. Conversions of garages into rooms, extensions and loft conversions will usually need planning permission. The rules are comprehensive. For example, fences over 2 metres in height need permission and where the fence will abut the street then any fence over 1 metre requires permission.

Many building societies or other lenders on properties, who have a vested interest in the property, need to give consent before building works are undertaken or a house is used to work from home.

Planning fees vary. The fee for an extension might be about £80.

Building regulations consent

Building regulations consent is needed separately from, and in addition to, planning permission. This consent is required for extensions and other changes to a home, and involves the checking and approval of plans, and the changes to the home to ensure that they are safe and properly built. Typical fees would be £27 for plan checking and £80 for inspection.

Rights of way and access

For most suburban properties issues concerning rights of way and access are unlikely to arise. However, those who live in isolated country properties may rely on a right of way to gain access to their land. When buying a property of that sort your solicitor should consider carefully what rights of access there are to your new property and also whether anyone else has a right of way over your land. Your beautiful country house may not appear as scenic if the local rambling club exercise their rights of access over your front lawn every weekend. It is possible to have public rights of way re-routed.

Rights of way can arise anew. Where a path is used for over 20 years then a right of way is acquired. A right known as 'adverse possession' can arise, where land is used for over 12 years by someone else without objection from the owner. The user can acquire title to the land. Even in towns this right can occur. If your neighbour builds a fence on your land and uses part of your garden for 12 years without objection from you, you could lose your rights to that land.

Rights in the air

You buy a house. How far up do your rights extend? You cannot prevent aeroplanes flying over the sky above you unless they fly extremely low. You could sue a neighbour who erects a sign which extends over your land for 'trespass' in the civil courts. Overhanging branches can be lopped off, but your neighbour will own the branches which you have cut down from his or her tree. Where the views from your property are spoilt there is no legal remedy, unless the other person has erected some structure without planning permission, where it was necessary to obtain such permission.

Trespass

Trespass is a civil wrong. Trespass occurs where someone comes on to your land without your consent. There is deemed consent for postmen etc to come on to your land, unless you erect a sign forbidding visitors. Trespassers cannot be 'prosecuted' since prosecution is a criminal action, which only the police or Crown Prosecution Service can bring where a crime is committed, for example if the person intruding on your land causes a breach of the peace or criminal damage. Trespassers can be sued in the civil courts, though, for the tort, or legal wrong, of trespass.

Disputes with neighbours

Most property disputes with neighbours concern:

- noise;
- smells;
- other nuisances;
- boundary or fencing disputes.

It is preferable if the dispute can be settled quickly. Many people are reluctant to complain to their neighbour until matters get out of hand. It can be better to complain when a nuisance begins, rather than have the neighbour believe, through your lack of complaints over the years, that you easily tolerate their pop music at 2am every morning. Speaking face to face and keeping cool can achieve more than losing your temper, which is likely to result in positions becoming entrenched.

A certain amount of noise has to be tolerated. You are unlikely to get very far complaining about lawnmower noise or crying babies, but loud arguments between husband and wife could be a justifiable cause for complaint. If your complaints do not result in a reduction in noise, smell or whatever, then consider reporting the matter to the local council and taking legal proceedings for nuisance. The legal wrong or tort of nuisance will only occur where there is a substantial and enduring nuisance. Gather evidence, take photographs, obtain statements from other neighbours, take video recordings. Then see a solicitor or the local Citizens' Advice Bureau or law centre for advice as to how to bring a claim.

The local council may bring its own proceedings under either statute law or local by-laws. There may, for example, be local by-laws concerning garden fires or the keeping of livestock, which might be the source of the nuisance. The environmental health officer may become involved or social workers, where, for example, a household keeps dozens of cats unhygienically and there are children in the home.

The Protection from Harassment Act 1997 can be used to stop some nuisance neighbours. Non-molestation orders can be obtained. Contact a solicitor for further information.

Fences

Where the deeds of a house do not specify who is responsible for the upkeep of fencing, then the fencing will be the responsibility of the neighbour on whose side the vertical support posts are fixed. The Party Wall Act 1996 changed the law in this area from 1 July 1997 so that anyone intending to carry out works on a party or shared wall or fence has to tell the adjoining owner and if the work causes damage then it must be made good. The Act also covers excavations near someone else's land. The Act gives rights to cut into shared structures to install damp proof courses and strengthen walls.

Dogs

Problems caused by neighbours' dogs include noise, which could amount to a legal nuisance as mentioned above and any damage they may do. Certain dogs, such as pit bull terriers, are required to be registered and insured under the Dangerous Dogs Act 1991. Otherwise there is no obligation now to register ownership of a dog. The Act also introduced an offence of having a dog out of control in a public place. Owners of dogs which bite may be prosecuted under this Act. Where the dog has never bitten before, it can be difficult for the authorities to require that the dog be put down. Further changes to the law are being considered.

If a dog is knocked down in the road there is a legal obligation to report the accident to the police. Dogs are required by law to wear a collar giving their owner's name and address, and the local authority can require that dogs be kept on leads in certain places.

Fouling of the footpath is likely to breach local by-laws and could also amount to the general crime of criminal damage. Private prosecutions could be brought in this area.

Settling disputes with neighbours

Anyone kept awake at night for hours on end by noisy music and revelling is unlikely to feel conciliatory. However, although you may lose your temper then, there can be merit in another personal visit the next day to talk things through. Perhaps a compromise is possible. The neighbour could restrict the number of parties and tell you in advance when one is to be held. They could invite you to the event or at least give you the opportunity to go away for the weekend.

Speaking calmly, but firmly, and suggesting compromise can get you further than shouting at the neighbour. Where the dispute cannot be solved amicably then legal advice will need to be taken and proceedings started. You may even prefer to move house!

Summary — property points

- An Englishman's home is not his castle. Always consider:
  — planning laws and building regulations;
  — your tenancy agreement;
  — your mortgage terms;
  — your lease;
  — restrictive covenants in relation to the property;
  — listed building consents;
  — conservation area restrictions;
  — local by-laws;
  — tax considerations of working from home.

- Resolve disputes with neighbours amicably where possible. The law will assist with the torts of trespass and nuisance. Complain to the local authority too.

12
Tax

Everyone has an obligation to pay tax. Many employees simply have tax deducted from their wages under the PAYE system by their employer, but any extra earnings, whether from letting a room in your house or part-time work in your spare time, should be declared to the Inland Revenue. It is necessary to ask the Inland Revenue to send you a tax return so that you can declare your extra income. Indeed, this may result in your being able to reclaim any tax over-paid. Note that it is untrue that just because you have never been sent a tax return by the Inland Revenue you are excused the obligation to pay tax. The onus is on you.

Avoidance and evasion

Tax avoidance is legal and evasion illegal. Tax avoidance is simply arranging your financial affairs to minimise the tax that you pay. For example, you may choose to become self-employed, because there are many expenses which you can set against your tax bill which are not tax deductible for employees. However, you cannot call yourself self-employed when you are not. The Inland Revenue look at all the circumstances and not how you describe yourself.

- Do you control why, where and how you work?
- Do you use your own tools and set your own hours?
- Are you responsible for paying tax? Do you pay VAT (value added tax)?
- Are you unpaid if you are sick or on holiday?
- Do you pay your own expenses?
- Do you undertake work for a number of different companies?

Other examples of lawful tax avoidance include maximising the use of income and capital gains tax allowances by the division of assets between husband and wife. For example, if one spouse pays a lower rate of tax than the other, or pays no tax at all, then it makes sense for building society accounts to be in that spouse's name. However, always beware of the 'tail wagging the dog' in tax avoidance. Such arrangement means that assets are being given to the other spouse. You lose control over them. There may be many reasons why this is a bad idea.

So, making maximum use of tax allowances, expenses rules, claiming tax refunds etc is fine. Tax evasion, on the other hand, is a crime. Tax evasion is simply not paying tax where it is due, usually deliberately. The most common scenarios are known to everyone. Mr X is claiming income support and decorating houses on the side. Miss Y has a full-time job and works for cash in a bar in the evenings. She does not tell the Inland Revenue that she has extra earnings from the bar work. Mrs Z earns money at car boot sales on a Saturday. She does not declare this income. This chapter looks at tax evasion and its consequences.

Inland Revenue investigations

The Inland Revenue is under a public duty to maximise tax revenues and ensure that those who pay tax on all their income are not subsidising those who do not. Also, inspectors are given targets to meet. More and more money is being recovered every year through Inland Revenue investigations. The Revenue is seeking to concentrate resources on 'complex and important accounts for investigation', but that does not mean that the tax evaders can relax.

Since April 1997, taxpayers with income other than simply that paid by an employer under PAYE have been sent a self-assessment tax return to complete. If you have income other than that from an employer, such as building society interest or income from casual work, then you will need to ask the Inland Revenue for a form and declare the income. It is an offence not to do so. It is no defence that the Inland Revenue never sent you the form. There are strict time limits for returning the form and you must keep evidence of business expenditure. The Inland Revenue have comprehensive telephone helplines to assist people with completion of the forms so there is no need to use an accountant. The Inland Revenue will calculate the tax due or the tax payer may do so if they wish.

The Inland Revenue will then pick on a proportion of returns to investigate each year even where there is nothing on the face of the return to suggest it is fraudulent. They intend to investigate the returns of those on higher incomes as these are a fruitful source for investigation.

There are routine exchanges of information between HM Customs and Excise (who handle VAT) and the Revenue. You are required to charge VAT where your business turnover is £49,000 per annum (the lower limit from 1 December 1997). It can be advantageous to register for VAT even when turnover is below the VAT threshold, as VAT paid can then be reclaimed.

Powers of the Inland Revenue

The Inland Revenue have powers to obtain papers and to search premises. Where you may have failed to comply with any provision of the Taxes Acts, ie where the Revenue suspects you have been dodging tax, they can serve a notice on you in writing to supply documents in your possession or in the possession of your spouse. You will have a period of at least 30 days to produce the information required. The Revenue typically would demand to see your account books and copies of bank statements. They have powers to go back over five years in investigations.

Before deciding whether to open a case for detailed investigation, the Revenue may visit your home to look for details as to your standard of living. You and your adviser (solicitor or accountant), if you have one, may be invited to attend an interview at the Revenue, where you will be told which areas of your affairs are causing them concern. There will then be a lengthy list of questions on all aspects of your business methods, and questions designed to show the level of your personal and private expenditure.

Notes will be taken at the interviews and you may be asked to sign a copy of the notes to confirm that they are complete. When attending such interviews be very careful what you say and always ask for a copy of any notes you sign. If there is anything wrong with the note, write to the Revenue confirming any inaccuracies.

After the interview there may be a visit to your business premises. You cannot refuse an inspection. The Revenue can obtain an entry warrant entitling them to enter premises. The Revenue may want to inspect any safe deposit box which you have at a bank. It may be at this stage that bank statements are requested, together with other books and records. Note that the Revenue has powers to require banks and third parties to hand over information.

Your role while this is going on is to convince the Revenue that your accounts are accurate or that you have no income which has not been declared. You may find it worth engaging an accountant or solicitor who has experience of tax investigations. There are likely to be negotiations with the Revenue and a settlement will be reached where it is clear that you have not declared all your income. There will be an appeal hearing where you appeal against any assessment raised against you. Where, for example, you have not declared sufficient income the Revenue may send a tax assessment based on the figures they think are right. It is then up to you to appeal that assessment.

Appeal hearings

You may represent yourself before the Inland Revenue Commissioners at an appeal hearing or appoint an accountant, solicitor or barrister. It will depend on your financial resources and the complexity of the case as to whether or not you represent yourself. The proceedings are a bit like court proceedings. Witnesses can be examined under oath. The Commissioners then reach their decision. There are rights of appeal.

Penalties

It is a criminal offence to hide, destroy or alter papers called for by the Revenue. Where you are found to have evaded tax then not only must you pay the additional tax you should have previously paid, but also an interest charge, ie interest on the sum due. This ensures that the Revenue is put in the same position as if it had been paid on time in the first place.

You will also have to pay a penalty. This can be negotiated with the Revenue, which is why it can be useful to use an adviser who has experience of such cases. This penalty will be a percentage of the tax under-paid.

Summary — tax

- Tax avoidance, arranging your affairs to minimise the tax you pay, is lawful.
- Tax evasion is against the law – declare all income to the Inland Revenue. Remember to include income from part-time work, income from investments, building society interest, dividends from shares etc, occasional income from car boot sales and the like.
- It is your responsibility to declare your income to the Inland Revenue by way of a self-assessment tax return. Keep full records of all your income and expenses, as this is required by law. If they do not send you a tax return and you have extra income, request one. You may be entitled to a tax refund.
- Register for VAT where your turnover exceeds £49,000 per annum.
- Reduce the risk of being investigated by submitting true and accurate accounts, if you run a business. Accounts showing much lower profits than other similar businesses will immediately catch the eye of the Revenue.
- Seek advice, if you can afford it, when you are investigated and be careful what you say or sign at an interview with a tax inspector.

13
Getting arrested

There are all sorts of reasons why the police might arrest you, eg for driving offences, pub brawls, shoplifting, drink and drugs, theft, burglary and muggings. This chapter considers some legal points which are common to all arrests.

You have no legal obligation to 'help the police with their enquiries', so the only way the police can force you to accompany them down to the police station is by arresting you. The police can arrest a suspect by obtaining an arrest warrant from a magistrate. The magistrate will have to be convinced that there is a case against the suspect.

The police also have powers of arrest without a warrant in the circumstances shown on the table below.

Powers of arrest without warrant

- An arrestable offence (ie one carrying a five-year potential jail sentence) has or could have been committed.
- Certain other specific offences have been committed such as rape, stealing cars, shoplifting or other theft offences, burglary, drug offences etc.
- If you are drunk or fail a breath test.
- If you are soliciting or living off immoral earnings.
- If you refuse to give your name and address where a particular law requires that you do so.
- Where a breach of the peace may occur or has occurred.

Citizens' arrests

Anyone can arrest another person where they commit any of the arrestable offences listed above. Therefore citizens who catch a bank robber in the street are making a legal arrest.

What to do if you are arrested

It may be possible to avoid being arrested by co-operating with the police in the first place. Answering questions which they wish to put to you might result in your convincing them that there is really no substance in their allegations.

However, if you are arrested then you should be informed of your right to see a solicitor. Even if it is the middle of the night, the duty solicitor scheme should mean that a solicitor will be on call and will speak to you over the telephone or come out to see you at the police station.

You should also be told that you have the right to inform some other person of your arrest. You could, therefore, call a relative or friend. You should be told that you have a right to look at the codes of practice followed by the police. You should be given a written note of the three rights above, which will also contain the usual caution that: '**You do not have to say anything, but it may harm your defence if you do not mention when questioned something which you later rely on in court. Anything you do say may be given in evidence**'.

This caution means the following.

- That you have a right of silence. You can choose to say nothing if you wish and it will be up to the prosecution to prove their case against you. In particular, you may choose to say nothing until your solicitor arrives. In very limited cases, such as high level share dealing investigations, the right of silence has been removed.
- What you say can be used in any legal proceedings which are brought. Although you may be able to prove that a 'confession' was beaten out of you, it is clearly much easier not to have confessed in the first place if you intend to plead not guilty at trial.

It is generally preferable to say nothing as you might end up admitting the offence or revealing details of your defence, which it would be better to save until the trial. Note that any interview is likely to be tape-recorded.

May the police detain you?

If you have not been arrested then the police cannot keep you at the police station. When you have been arrested you should be charged with an offence within 24 hours (usually) or released.

What happens next?

Assuming that you are charged with an offence you will probably already have seen a solicitor. If not, it is wise to do so. They will inform you in detail of the procedure and whether or not to plead guilty to the offence. After you are charged you will either be remanded on bail or in custody. If you are remanded in custody you will not be released until after the trial. Bail applications should not be refused unnecessarily, though you may need to find sureties and comply with conditions such as reporting regularly to the police station.

More minor offences are tried in the magistrates' courts and more serious offences in the Crown Court. Some offences are 'triable either way' and you have a choice.

You will need to prepare your case with your solicitor for the trial. There may be witnesses to find and statements to take. It is wise to practise how you will answer difficult questions if you decide to take the witness stand yourself.

At the trial you will be found guilty or not guilty. If you are found not guilty there may be grounds for you to bring proceedings against the police for false imprisonment arising from your original arrest. Consult a solicitor on this. If you are found guilty you will be sentenced and it is only at that stage that any previous convictions will be brought to light. Your solicitor may be able to put forward various facts in mitigation and sentencing might be delayed for welfare, medical or other reports to be prepared.

A criminal record

Once you have been convicted you will have a criminal record. Some offences are so minor that this does not really matter. Many people are convicted of minor driving offences such as speeding and these are unlikely to affect their future employment prospects or ability to obtain insurance, credit and mortgages etc. Also, your conviction can become 'spent', ie the slate is wiped clean and you do not need to reveal the conviction, after a certain period of time. Where you have been sent to prison for over two-and-a-half years your conviction will never be spent in this way. It takes ten years for a lesser prison sentence to be spent. Periods vary, so seek legal advice.

Even a minor motoring offence could have an impact on your life. A driving ban may lose you your job and even road accidents where no prosecution results can lead to your losing your no claims bonus on your car insurance.

Victims

So far, this chapter has concerned itself with the perpetrators of crime. You may find yourself on the receiving end of a criminal act, as a victim. Consider whether you wish to give evidence in court. It may be necessary for a conviction.

You may be able to claim compensation from your attacker – criminal courts will award compensation to victims and/or from the Criminal Injuries Compensation Authority (address in Sources of Further Information at the end of this book). In addition, once the criminal proceedings have been successfully concluded you might like to consider suing your attacker for damages. You can do this whether or not the police prosecute, but it is easier if you have the weight of a criminal prosecution behind you. It is wise to consult a solicitor. A claim for damages for loss suffered, as well as personal suffering etc, can be formulated and civil proceedings begun.

Always bear in mind, though, that your attacker may be very poor so you may have no prospect of recovering any money.

Summary — getting arrested

- When you are arrested consult a solicitor.
- Ensure that you are aware of your rights on arrest.
- Be cautious as to what you say and sign.
- Do not panic, keep cool and do not be violent or disrespectful to the police.
- Contact a solicitor and a friend or family member before saying anything.
- Exercise your right of silence until you have taken legal advice.
- Ensure that if you are charged a bail application is made.
- Prepare carefully for trial.
- Check when your criminal record will be 'spent'.
- If you are a victim, consider whether you wish to give evidence and what rights to compensation you might have.

14

Employment – the legal issues

The law affects employees and employers in a number of ways. There are legal obligations owed by the employer to the employee and vice versa. This chapter describes the legal position where an employee is taken on, during their employment and when they are sacked or made redundant.

Taking on a new job

When you take on a new job you are entitled to written particulars setting out certain terms of your employment. Your employer does not have to prepare a written contract of employment, provided you are given these written particulars. These written particulars must be supplied within 13 weeks of beginning a new job. The written particulars will include:

- names of employer and employee;
- date when the job began and whether any previous job counts towards the length of time worked in this job;
- pay and working hours;
- place of work;
- holidays;
- sick pay;
- pensions;
- complaints and disciplinary proceedings;
- termination of the employment contract.

Although these written particulars set out the main terms, it is better to have a written contract. Some employees, however, are faced with an 'employer' who wants to pay them cash and have no written record of their employment. Clearly those are the jobs to avoid. It is much harder to enforce your employment rights if you have nothing in writing. Where the employer does not present the written particulars, despite your requesting them, consider sending the employer a letter and keep a copy, setting out what your understanding of the terms which you have agreed is. At least that might help if there is a dispute about what pay, for example, had been agreed.

If you are self-employed or work part time there will be no obligation to supply the written particulars. In deciding whether you are truly self-employed or not, look at the 'control' factors described in Chapter 12 (page 70).

Changes in contract conditions

Can your employer change the contract you have agreed? If the employer proposes to reduce your pay that would need to be agreed, otherwise it would amount to a breach of contract by the employer. However, if you are presented with the proposal that either you accept a pay reduction, or staff will be laid off or the company go into liquidation, you may feel forced to agree to the change. Consider consulting a solicitor or your union, if you have one, in such circumstances. If you agree, then your employer can alter any of the terms of your contract.

Some minor changes are unlikely to amount to a breach of contract. However, requiring that you work abroad, relocate to a distant part of the country or work longer hours can amount to a breach of contract by the employer, depending on your original contract of employment. Usually the choice is to accept the change or be paid off.

Where the business for which you work is sold off then the new employer takes on obligations from the old as to redundancy and unfair dismissal. The European Commission's Acquired Rights Directive resulted in the Transfer of Undertakings (Protection of Employment) Regulations 1981. It is these regulations which preserve employment rights where there is a transfer of a business. Seek legal advice if you are laid off as a result of a merger, takeover or acquisition.

There are many obligations which employers owe to employees, including complying with various health and safety laws. One of the difficulties which employees have is the inequality of bargaining power. In times where unemployment is high and other jobs hard to find, drawing your employer's attention to breaches of health and safety legislation is unlikely to endear you to him or her. However, if your health is at risk you should consider a complaint. Much can be gained by tact and making the right approach to ensure that your complaint is received in a spirit of co-operation, rather than anger. Suggest solutions, rather than simply drawing attention to problems.

Smoking at work

Breathing the cigarette smoke of others can damage your health. Employers are increasingly realising that they could be liable for civil actions for damages where they allow employees to suffer in this way. If you are a smoker and are told that a smoking ban is being imposed you may feel you have to leave your job. Whether or not you will have a claim for unfair dismissal will depend on all the circumstances. Some employers set aside smoking rooms, offer counselling or allow smokers regular breaks to go outside to smoke.

Discrimination and maternity rights

Where you face discrimination at work on the grounds of sex or race or, in certain cases, disability, you can bring a claim before an industrial tribunal. It is wise to consult with a solicitor, law centre or Citizens' Advice Bureau first. There is no law against discriminating on the grounds of age.

Most women have rights to time off to have a baby and not to be dismissed by reason of pregnancy. Check carefully the time limits and rights to maternity pay you might have. Free leaflets on maternity benefits are available from the DSS (see Sources of Further Information) and post offices.

Unfair dismissal and redundancy

Your contract of employment may state what period of notice the employer can give you to terminate your employment. If not, the law gives you a minimum period of notice. If you have been employed for under a month then no notice need be given. One week's notice must be given where you have been employed for between one month and two years, and thereafter one week for each year of employment. A year is a full year. This continues to a maximum of 12 weeks' notice at 12 years.

If you are dismissed without notice then you can bring a claim for wrongful dismissal against the employer for your wages in that notice period. For example, if you have a contract which can be terminated on one month's notice and your employer sacks you without notice, assuming you have done nothing wrong, then you can sue for a month's wages.

In addition, you might be able to bring a claim before an industrial tribunal for unfair dismissal or redundancy, provided that you have been employed for two years by your employer. When seeking a new job be careful to remember the following:

- Ensure that you do not use confidential information of your employer, or material protected by copyright (such as computer programs) or patents, customer lists etc in your new job or in setting up a new business. If you do you could be sued.
- Stick to 'restrictive covenants' in your contract of employment. Those covenants may restrict you from carrying on a similar business within a certain geographical area. Seek legal advice if you propose to do this as the covenants may be unenforceable if they are too broad and there may be ways round your employer's other rights.

In bringing a claim for unfair dismissal or redundancy, the first stage is to determine whether or not you are eligible and then to ascertain whether or not you were fairly dismissed. If you have been stealing from the employer or are repeatedly absconding from the work place or are incompetent at the job etc, then you are unlikely to have any claim.

Industrial tribunals

Industrial tribunals were set up 30 years ago as informal proceedings for the settlement of employment disputes. Unlike the courts, each side pays their own costs. You may use a union official or friend to represent you.

Claims must be made within three months of dismissal or redundancy.

If you are sacked you have a right to obtain from your employer written reasons for your dismissal and this should be the first step you take in pursuing your claim. It is then necessary to obtain a form from the industrial tribunal and complete this with details of your claim.

The employer is sent a copy by the tribunal and the employer completes a further form in response.

You will be entitled to call witnesses at the hearing and will be given 14 days' notice of the hearing date. Prepare your case carefully and ensure that you have copies of all relevant documentation, such as your contract of employment and any correspondence with the employer.

The tribunal, if it upholds your claim, can make an award of compensation, comprising a basic award and a compensatory award. Awards are generally low – one or two thousand pounds – though sums up to £11,300 can be awarded. The European Court of Justice in 1993 held that the UK's statutory upper limits for compensation in relation to sex discrimination claims are unlawful and anyone in such cases should seek legal advice on whether a legal maximum still applies in their case.

The tribunal can also order that you be reinstated (given your job back), but this is rarely ordered. The tribunal will usually come to the conclusion that the acrimony involved in a claim of this sort means that it would be impracticable to expect the employer to take the ex-employee back.

A redundancy payment will be made where an employee is dismissed because of redundancy. If you are made redundant then that is regarded as a 'fair' reason to dismiss you, so no claim to unfair dismissal is possible, although you will be entitled to redundancy payments. If your employer has hired a replacement then you are more likely to have been dismissed than made redundant. What sum you receive on redundancy is set by statute, although many firms offer more generous terms. The statutory sum is based on the number of years in employment with that employer.

Action plan on dismissal

The table below describes some of the steps you should take to protect your legal position if you are made redundant or dismissed.

Action plan on dismissal

- Discuss the decision. You might be able to convince the employer to change their mind or negotiate a better leaving package. Discuss:
  - (a) arrears of salary;
  - (b) accrued holiday pay;
  - (c) outstanding expenses claims;
  - (d) company cars/telephones etc, whether you can keep them or when they should be returned;
  - (e) pension position;
  - (f) admit nothing concerning your past conduct and sign no pieces of paper without legal advice.
- Collect all your belongings before you go.
- Collect a cheque there and then, if possible, for all sums owed to cover (a) to (c) above, or any other money.
- Collect your P45.
- Ask your employer for written reasons for dismissal. You need to ascertain why you were dismissed. Was it redundancy or unfair dismissal?
- Consider whether you have a legal claim against your employer. Look at all documentation, letter of dismissal, contract of employment, reasons for dismissal etc. Consult ex-colleagues whom you can trust, friends and take legal advice from the Citizens' Advice Bureau, law centre or solicitor.
- Keep a careful record of what your employer said and write down a history of your difficulties with the employer, examples of sexual harassment or whatever the circumstances were which led to the dismissal.
- Within three months of dismissal bring your claim for unfair dismissal in an industrial tribunal. Bring a claim for wrongful dismissal, too, where you have not been given notice of the correct period of termination of your contract of employment. Your employer may offer to pay you compensation in lieu of notice. This will usually be tax free up to £30,000, unless your contract of employment gives the employer the right to pay you instead of giving notice of dismissal.
- Prepare well for the hearing and consider whom you might call as witnesses.
- In taking a new job or setting up in business, be careful not to breach restrictive covenants in your contract of employment, or use or disclose confidential information of your employer, or act in breach of copyright or other intellectual property rights of the employer.

15
Faulty goods

Few people are able to avoid buying faulty goods. This chapter considers your legal rights and remedies where goods you have purchased do not come up to standard.

The contract of sale

Every time that you buy goods in a shop you are entering into a legal contract, even though there may be nothing written down. The Sale of Goods Act 1979 implies certain terms and conditions into that contract, and it is these terms which give you your basic legal rights when faulty goods are purchased. In addition, you may have specific rights to cancel certain consumer contracts under the Consumer Credit Act 1974. This gives you rights to change your mind within a certain period of buying goods on credit. The company concerned should tell you of your rights in that area and further information can be obtained from the Office of Fair Trading (details can be found in Sources of Further Information at the end of this book).

Any goods you buy must be of satisfactory quality and fit for the purpose for which they were intended. There are implied terms that the seller has the right to sell the goods, ie that they are his or hers to sell, and that the goods are as the seller has described them, where there is a 'sale by description', as there might be where goods are sold sight unseen by post.

Second-hand goods

Where do you stand on these implied terms if the goods are bought second-hand? The implied terms still apply, although you cannot expect the goods to be of the same quality as new goods. However, the implied terms only apply to contracts where one party is in business. Someone selling you their car through the small ads in the local paper will not be taken to warrant that the goods are of merchantable quality.

There is no reason why you cannot, in all situations, negotiate express terms about the goods. Indeed, many business contracts are negotiated in this way. Have the seller write down and sign that the car, or whatever product, has 'only had one driver', or has been regularly serviced or has a new engine, or whatever you are concerned about. That way you can sue for breach of contract if the facts turn out to be different. You may even be able to sue for 'misrepresentation' where untrue statements are made about the goods.

Exclusion of liability

Many standard contracts for the sale of goods, where there are written terms of business, contain a clause limiting the liability of the seller to the purchaser. The seller may agree only to make an attempt to put any problem right and limit total compensation. Such contract terms generally are only enforceable to the extent that they are 'reasonable' under the Unfair Contract Terms Act 1977 and provided they are not unfair under the Unfair Terms in Consumer Contracts Regulations 1994. The Office of Fair Trading has an unfair terms unit to which complaints can be made.

Dangerous products

Where you are damaged by a product, for example poisoned or cut, you will have a claim for breach of contract where the seller expressly or impliedly warranted the quality of the goods. However, if you are not the purchaser then you would not be able to sue under the contract.

Only the parties to a contract, ie buyer and seller, can sue for breach of contract

However, you may be able to sue for the tort, or legal wrong, of 'negligence', where you can show that the supplier owed you a duty of care and had acted in breach of that duty.

The Consumer Protection Act 1987 imposes what is known as 'strict liability' on suppliers for their products where the products cause physical injury or damage. This means that you could sue the supplier, the importer or the company whose trade mark appears on the goods where there is a defect in the goods.

Getting compensation

When you buy faulty goods consider approaching the situation in the following way.

Getting compensation for faulty goods

- Are the goods faulty? Consider getting an expert's report where the goods were very expensive.
- Get together all documentation and make a note of the date of purchase. Do you have the receipt, guarantee and instruction booklet? Examine these.
- If the goods are covered by a guarantee this 'will not affect your statutory rights' — this means that if the guarantee offers a replacement product for, say, six months after purchase and the product breaks down in a year's time, you may still be able to obtain damages if it is reasonable to expect that a product of that sort would operate for a longer period and therefore the implied term that the product will be of satisfactory quality could be enforced.
- However, if the guarantee still applies, claim under that.
- Contact the seller (not the manufacturer as your contract is with the retailer) where you bought the goods.
- State your case clearly, on the telephone or at the shop first, then in writing if a visit or telephone call does not result in action. Chapter 5 gives a sample letter you might send in such cases.
- Before suing, try contacting someone higher up in the company or the manufacturer.
- Where all else fails, sue. Chapter 5 shows how to go about bringing a claim in the small claims court, but consider carefully whether the hassle and expense are justified when taking into account the amount of your loss.

16
Wills and probate

This chapter describes the law relating to death. Most people at some stage of their lives have to deal not only with the emotional trauma, but also with the legal side of death.

Dying without making a will

You can make things much easier for your family if you prepare a will. The purpose of a will is to make it clear to whom your goods will go when you die.

Consequences of dying intestate

If you die without a will then you are 'intestate':

- the law decides who gets what;
- if you leave a spouse and children, your spouse receives a fixed sum of £75,000 (if there is that much available) and half the balance over that figure for life and all the personal effects, and the children and grandchildren receive the other half;
- if there are no relatives except the spouse he/she receives everything;
- if there is no spouse or children, the parents inherit, but if they are dead then brothers and sisters inherit.

This is just a short summary of the main rules. As can be seen, dying without making a will can be complicated and could result, for example, in a spouse having to share assets and income with the children, where the deceased partner might have wanted their partner to inherit everything.

Making a will

You do not need a solicitor to draw up a will, although a solicitor's charges for wills are usually modest and you are less likely to make major mistakes which can result in invalidating a will if you employ a solicitor. Law stationers (details in Sources of Further Information) and other stationery shops sell model wills which are generally acceptable, but it is preferable if legal advice is obtained.

Your will will deal with who inherits what in your 'estate', ie what you own. Unless you have valuable antiques there is no need to produce an endless list of individual 'legacies', ie gifts, for example, Aunt Mabel gets the furry tea cosy, although there is nothing to stop you doing so if you wish.

The main points to cover are to state who inherits the bulk of your estate. You can leave your assets to whomever you choose, although people supported by you, under the Inheritance (Provision for Family and Dependants) Act 1975, may be able to make a claim against your estate if you leave them nothing.

Your will can also deal with who are appointed guardians of your children when you and your spouse die. The proposed guardians should be asked first as taking on someone else's children is a considerable burden.

Individuals will be appointed 'executors' under your will. That means they are in charge of obtaining the 'grant of probate' and administering your estate, ie handing out the money and preparing the accounts. Probate is the document issued as official evidence of the executor's authority. Often a solicitor is appointed to this role. An executor can be a relative or someone who will inherit under the will. Solicitors and banks will make charges for their services in this connection. Your will may also specify your preferred burial or cremation arrangements.

When drafting a will do not assume that your assets now will be the same on death. It is much better to give specific legacies, say a few hundred pounds to godchildren or others and then specify that the 'residue', ie the rest, whatever sum that may comprise at death, will go to your main beneficiary, say your spouse, and if he or she is dead, to your children. Deal with inheritance tax and be clear in the terms you use to describe your property.

Will formalities

Your will will not be valid if you do not sign it in the presence of two witnesses, who must also sign the will. Witnesses cannot be beneficiaries under the will. The will can be in handwriting, but is easier to read if it is typed. It is important to let others know where the will can be found, in case you die and no one knows of the will's existence.

Changing and revoking wills

When you divorce or marry your will is automatically revoked (ie invalidated), so always prepare a new will in those circumstances. Otherwise, a will can be changed at any time. Where substantial changes are to be made it is best to draw up a new will, making clear in the will that the new will revokes previous wills. Always ensure that a will is dated. If very small changes are to be made these can be done by means of a 'codicil'. This document should confirm all other terms of the original will, except the change effected in the codicil. The formalities for executing a will need to be followed in executing a codicil.

Death

When someone dies, a death certificate will be provided by a doctor. Where the deceased is an organ donor, the local hospital should be informed and if they are religious then a priest (or other representative – depending on the person's religion) should be called. Where the death is violent or suspicious then a coroner may require that an inquest be held.

As with marriages and births, deaths must be registered with the Registrar of Births, Marriages and Deaths. Funeral arrangements must be dealt with, and there will also be people to notify and all sorts of administrative tasks to do, such as informing banks, finding life insurance policies and, for the executors appointed under any will, sorting out the estate. Application must be made for a grant of probate and the deceased's financial affairs sorted out. This can take time as properties may need to be sold and tax assessments agreed. Where the estate's value exceeds £215,000 (for the tax year 1997/8) inheritance tax is payable at a rate of 40 per cent on the excess, subject to various reliefs. Obtain professional advice about these.

Summary — wills and probate

- Always consider making a will, even if you are single.
- Ensure that the will is properly drawn up and that you observe the legal formalities. It is best to employ a solicitor for this.
- Marriage and divorce automatically revoke wills so prepare a new will on these occurrences.
- If you die without a will you are said to be 'intestate' and the State determines, according to fixed rules, who inherits what.
- You are free, in a will, to leave your property to whomever you prefer, but dependants may have a legal claim for some part of your estate. You can, however, leave it to them to apply for such support on your death.
- When someone dies, a death certificate from a doctor should be obtained and the Registrar of Births, Marriages and Deaths informed. The estate of the deceased will then be sorted out and eventually the assets dispersed.

17
Other legal areas

There are all sorts of other areas where the law affects people's lives. This book has concentrated on those legal areas most frequently affecting the average person. There follows a brief summary of some more legal areas, but there are many others.

Libel and slander

Legal actions can be brought for libel or slander where untruths which damage your reputation are, in the case of libel, written or, in case of slander, spoken. The communication of the untruth must be to a third party. If someone writes you a letter describing you as a 'marriage wrecker' or an 'incompetent electrician' there will be no libel since only you will see the letter. If they send the letter to the local newspaper you may be able to sue the writer and the newspaper. Bear in mind, though, that such actions can involve substantial legal costs.

Intellectual property law

If you write a literary, artistic or dramatic work, such as a book or computer software, you will have produced a work protected by copyright, under the Copyright, Designs and Patents Act 1988. However, if the work is produced during the course of your employment your employer will own the copyright, unless you agree to the contrary. You can sell (assign) your copyright to someone else for a lump sum or give others permission to use it (a licence).

If you invent something you may be able to apply for a patent under the Patents Act 1977. Details of the Patent Office to whom applications should be made appear in Sources of Further Information. Similarly, registered designs can be protected and some functional designs are protected without the need for registration as design rights, under the 1988 Act mentioned above. Again, these rights can be sold or licensed to others, or you can use them yourself for business purposes. Your employer will own rights to those inventions you make as part of your job. Seek legal advice in cases of doubt.

If you run a business you are highly likely to use a trade name. You may wish to register a trade mark at the Trade Marks Registry (see details in Sources of Further Information). Also, if others copy your business 'get up', such as your business logo or design, then you may be able to sue for the tort or legal wrong of 'passing off'.

Confidential data

There is a large body of law concerning confidential information and its protection. Anyone holding personal data on computer, such as details of customers, is obliged to register under the Data Protection Act 1984 and give individual 'data subjects' access to such information. Details of the Data Protection Register appear in Sources of Further Information.

There are rules and regulations concerning unsolicited mail. If goods arrive which you have not ordered, under the Unsolicited Goods and Services Act 1971 the goods must be retained for six months in case the sender wishes to retrieve them in that period. You are not obliged to return them. If you want the matter sorted out sooner, though, you may write to the sender of the goods notifying them of their arrival. If you receive no response within 30 days, you may retain the goods free of charge, unless the seller responds within the 30-day period. Anyone suffering from cold calling and other indirect selling practices will find their rights improved when the 1997 EU distance contracts directive 97/7 comes into force by 20 May 2000.

There are also regulations regulating the mail order sector, such as the Mail Order Protection Scheme. Various codes of advertising practice also apply and if you see an advertisement which is misleading you can report it to the Advertising Standards Authority (details in Sources of Further Information).

Competition law

Those operating a business need to be aware that entering into restrictive agreements or exploiting their position of market power could lead them to fall foul of the Restrictive Trade Practices Act 1976 or the Competition Act 1980 (both to be replaced in 1998 by a new tougher Competition Act) or EC competition legislation in Articles 85 and 86 of the Treaty of Rome.

Restrictions in employment contracts may be held unenforceable where they are unreasonable. They are described as being 'in restraint of trade' because they stop an individual carrying on a business. Whether a clause is reasonable depends on how wide the employer has drafted it. In the UK, the Office of Fair Trading is in charge of competition law, but restrictive covenants are a matter for the courts.

Foreign legal systems

Each country's laws differ from those abroad. If you are in trouble abroad you will need to seek legal advice there from a local expert. You may be offered assistance by your travel company, if you are on a package holiday, or the British Consul in the territory concerned.

When doing business with foreign customers or companies, areas of law such as 'choice of law and jurisdiction', ie which country's law applies and where any legal proceedings should be brought, become relevant. There are various international conventions which assist in determining these issues.

Many other laws

'The law' comprises a vast body of statutes, cases and regulations, some emanating from the courts and parliament, and others from the European Commission. From the European Convention on Human Rights to misleading advertising regulations, regulations concerning seat belts and TV licences to immigration law, the law regulates society, business and individuals. Its complexity results from the complexity of the society from which it has developed.

However, many of the basic laws of the land are simple in concept – prohibitions on murder and theft, etc. Where complex issues arise legal advice is usually available, although the principal difficulty for many is the cost of it. Solicitors are often beyond the means of anyone ineligible for Legal Aid or without vast resources. This book has described the principal areas of law with which most people need to be concerned. It has also indicated where free legal advice may be available.

Justice is never perfect, but the British legal system, for all its faults, is admired the world over and has been used as a model in many States. It is only by individuals enforcing their rights that our system of justice continues and only by knowledge of such rights that individuals have the ability to ensure such enforcement.

Legal terms

affidavit A sworn statement used in legal cases, sworn in front of a solicitor or commissioner for oaths.

arbitration The process of settling a dispute without going to court, can be through trade associations or by using a member of the Institute of Arbitrators. The process is secret, unlike court proceedings which are open. Arbitration is normally fairly formal and lawyers are used. The Arbitration Act 1996 covers this area.

assignment A transfer of rights, eg copyright or patents, or transferring the benefit of rights under a contract.

bailiff Someone used by the court to enforce a judgment by entering premises and taking goods for sale to settle a judgment debt.

bankruptcy State where an individual is declared to be unable to pay creditors by the court.

barrister An advocate who represents clients in court and is admitted as a barrister by the Bar Council.

beneficiary Someone who benefits under a will by being left property or other assets.

charge A right over the property of another person, usually in exchange for a loan. Default on the loan results in a right to sell the charged property.

chattels Property other than real property (land and buildings) – thus, things.

codicil Amendment to a will.

consideration Money or other gain from which someone benefits under a contract to make it enforceable.

costs Legal expenses which may be paid in a legal action, solicitors' fees.

counterclaim A pleading submitted by a defendant, where he or she wishes to claim against the plaintiff.

counterfeit products Goods made in breach of the rights such as trade marks and patents of another maker, such as fake exclusive name watches or perfume.

deed A formal legal document which is signed, sealed and delivered (although sealing is no longer required).

defence The pleading put in by the defendant setting out why the defendant contests a legal action brought against him or her.

defendant The person defending a legal action.

discovery A stage in a legal action where each party to the action reveals documents which they have concerning the case to the other party.

estate Property left by a deceased person on their death.

executors Individuals appointed under a will to undertake the administrative task of disposing of assets etc required under a will.

freehold Owning real property outright, as opposed to by way of leasehold.

garnishee order A court order allowing a debtor rights over the bank account or other money of a defendant.

indictable offence A serious criminal offence which must be tried in the Crown Court.

injunction A court order restraining someone from doing something, eg a violent husband from going near his wife or a counterfeiter from selling counterfeit products.

insolvency A company unable to pay its debts as they fall due under insolvency legislation – the Insolvency Act 1986.

intestate Dying without making a will.

leasehold Owning property under a lease, with a requirement to surrender the property to the freeholder at the end of the lease.

legacy A gift under a will.

licence (1) A permission to use, eg permission to occupy a property without a lease or tenancy agreement, or permission to use a patent or trade mark and (2) permission from the court or licensing authorities, such as is required for forms of street trading or to sell liquor etc.

liquidation Formal legal state of a company once declared unable to pay its debts.

litigation Legal actions in the courts.

novation Arrangement to allow one party to a contract to drop out and a new party take its place, needs signature by all three parties, and is the method of transferring all rights and obligations under a contract, *see also* assignment.

particulars of claim Details of a claim in a legal action either on a summons form or a separate form where county court proceedings are brought.

passing off A tort or legal wrong under which the wrongdoer holds out his or her business as being that of, or connected to, the business of another.

personal representatives Individuals appointed to tie up the estate of someone who has died without making a will.

plaintiff A person bringing a legal action.

pleadings Documents used in a legal action – a general term to describe a statement of claim, defence, counterclaim etc.

precedent (1) A previous decision of the courts which 'binds' other courts in later decisions, ie in future such cases the courts must decide in the same way; (2) a sample standard contract, for example for a lease or other legal agreement, which is used as a starting point in drafting another similar document.

probate A document issued authorising executors under a will to proceed with settling the estate.

real property Land and buildings.

solicitor A legal adviser to clients, admitted as a solicitor of the Supreme Court by the Law Society.

statement of claim Details of a claim endorsed on a writ, setting out the plaintiff's case.

statutory instrument A regulation made by parliament.

testator Someone who makes a will.

title Ownership, usually of land.

trustee in bankruptcy An insolvency practitioner (accountant) appointed to administer the estate of a bankrupt.

vendor Seller.

void Unenforceable.

writ A document issued by the High Court to initiate a legal action.

Note: These are the principal legal terms used. However, there are many others. Further information on legal terms is contained in the *Oxford Dictionary of Law* (1997 edn, Oxford).

Sources of further information

Sources of free legal advice and funding

Citizens' Advice Bureaux, Head Office, Middleton House, 115–123 Pentonville Road, London N1 9LZ; 0171 833 2181

Law Centres Federation, Duchess House, 18–19 Warren Street, W1P 5DB; 0171 387 8570

Legal Advice Centres, The Law Society, 113 Chancery Lane, London WC2A 1PL; 0171 242 1222

The Legal Aid Board London Area Office, 29/37 Red Lion Street, London WC1R 4PP; 0171 813 5300

Government bodies

Data Protection Registrar (data held on computer, access rights, misuse of data, credit blacklisting etc), Wycliffe House, Water Lane, Wilmslow, Cheshire SK9 5AF; 01625 535777

Department for Education (for education queries), Century Building, Great Smith Street, Westminster, London SW1P 3BT; 0171–925 5000

Department of Health (NHS etc) and Department of Social Security (income support, family credit etc), Richmond House, 79 Whitehall, London SW1A 2NS; 0171 210 3000

Department of Trade and Industry (business advice), Ashdown House, 123 Victoria Street, London SW1E 6RB; 0171 215 5000

Office of Fair Trading (consumer and competition law enquiries), Field House, 15/25 Bream's Buildings, London EC4R 1PR; 0171 242 2858

The Patent Office (patents and registered designs) and the Trade Mark Office (trade marks), Concert House, Cardiff Road, Newport, Gwent NP9 1RH; 0633 814000

Ombudsmen

For complaints in relation to the relevant industry listed below:

Banking Ombudsman, 70 Gray's Inn Road, London WC1X 8NB; 0171 404 9944

Building Societies' Ombudsman, Grosvenor Gardens House, 35/37 Grosvenor Gardens, London SW1X 7AW; 0171 931 0044

Corporate Estate Agents' Ombudsman, Suite 3, Old Library Chambers, Chipper Lane, Salisbury, Wiltshire SP1 1YQ; 01722 333306

Health Service Ombudsman, Church House, Great Smith Street, London SW1P 3BW; 0171 276 3000

Independent Housing Ombudsman (for the protection of housing association tenants against landlord mismanagement), Norman House, 105–9 The Strand, London WC2R 0AA; 0171 836 3630

Insurance Ombudsman, City Gate One, 135 Park Street, London SE1 9EA; 0171 928 4488

Legal Services' Ombudsman, 22 Oxford Court, Oxford Street, Manchester M2 3WQ; 0161 236 9532

Local Government Ombudsman – London, 21 Queen Anne's Gate, London SW1H 9BU; 0171 915 3210

There are other regional local government ombudsmen

Pensions Ombudsman, 11 Belgrave Road, London SW1V 1RB; 0171 834 9144

Utilities bodies

For complaints concerning the relevant industry:

OFGAS (gas), Stockley House, 130 Wilton Road, London SW1V 1LQ; 0171 828 0898

OFTEL (telephones), 50 Ludgate Hill, London EC4M 7JJ; 0171 634 8700

OFWAT (water), 15–17 Ridgmount Street, London WC1E 7AH; 0171 636 3656

OFFER (electricity), 2nd Floor, 11 Belgrave Road, London SW1V 1RB; 0171 233 6366

Associations

Consumers' Association, 2 Marylebone Road, London NW1 4DX; 0171 486 5544

Advertising Standards Authority, Brook House, 2–16 Torrington Place, London WC1E 7HN; 0171 580 5555

Bodies regulating the professions

For complaints about their members or details of how to find a solicitor, accountant etc.

Accountants

The Institute of Chartered Accountants of England and Wales, PO Box 433, Chartered Accountants' Hall, Moorgate Place, London EC2P 2BJ; 0171 920 8100

The Institute of Chartered Accountants of Scotland, 27 Queen Street, Edinburgh EH2 ILA; 0131 225 5673

Architects

The Architects' Registration Council of the United Kingdom (ARCUK), 73 Hallam Street, London W1N 6EE; 0171 580 5861

The Royal Institute of British Architects, 66 Portland Place, London W1N 4AD; 0171 580 5533

Patent and trade mark agents

The Chartered Institute of Patent Agents, Staple Inn Buildings, High Holborn, London WC1V 7PZ; 0171 405 9450

The Institute of Trade Mark Agents, 6th Floor, Canterbury House, 2–6 Sydenham Road, Croydon CR0 9XE; 0181 686 2052

Solicitors

The Law Society, 113 Chancery Lane, London WC2A 1PL; 0171 242 1222

Complaints about solicitors should be sent to:

The Office for the Supervision of Solicitors, Victoria Court, 8 Dormer Place, Leamington Spa, Warwickshire CV32 5AE; 0926 822007

Various commercial guides to professional advisers are available including the following.

Chambers and Partners' Directory, ed M. Chambers, Chambers and Partners Publishing, 74 Long Lane, London EC1A 9ET; 0171 606 2266, published annually. It attempts an evaluation not only of firms, but also individual solicitors, showing their particular expertise and areas of specialisation.

The Legal 500, J. Pritchard, Legalease, 28–33 Cato Street, London W1H 5HS; 0171 396 9292, published annually. Lists solicitors' firms and evaluates their expertise.

The Institute of Chartered Accountants in England and Wales Directory of Firms, available from the Institute of Chartered Accountants (address above). Lists accountants.

Getting Value from Professional Advisers, by Catriona Standish, Kogan Page, 1993; 0171 278 0433. Advises on how to find and keep good professional advisers, and keep their costs down.

Family and children

Various counselling organisations can offer help and support for those experiencing family problems, including the following.

Relate (formerly the Marriage Guidance Council) – contact local branches through *Yellow Pages*

National Association of Family Mediation and Conciliation Services, Shaftsbury Centre, Percy Street, Swindon, Wiltshire SN2 2AZ; 01793 514055

Divorce, Conciliation and Advisory Service, 38 Ebury Street, London SW1W 0LU; 0171 730 2422

One Parent Families, 255 Kentish Town Road, London NW5; 0171 267 1361

Families Need Fathers, 134 Curtain Street, London EC2A 3AR; 0171 613 5060

Family Mediators Association, The Old Rectory Gardens, Henbury, Bristol BS10 7AQ; 01272 500140 and 0181 954 6383

The Child Support Agency pursues maintenance claims against absent parents. Enquiry line 0345 133133

There are many registered charities dedicated to particular problem areas. Details can be obtained from the Charity Commission, St Alban's House, 57–60 Haymarket, London SW1Y 4QX; 0171 210 3000

Copies of birth, marriage and death certificates can be obtained from the General Register Office, St Catherine's House, 10 Kingsway, London WC2B 6JP; 0171 242 0262

Details of the Adopted Children's Contact Register can be obtained from General Register Office, Adoption Section, Smedley Hydro, Trafalgar Road, Southport, Merseyside PR8 2HH; 0151 471 4831

When registering a birth, death or marriage the local registry details can be found in the *Yellow Pages* or by telephoning the local authority.

Records of divorces and probate/wills can be obtained from the Principal Registry, Family Division, Somerset House, Strand, London WC2R 1LP; Divorce: 0171 936 6000; Probate: 0171 936 6983

Criminal matters

Information on compensation for criminal injuries can be obtained from the Criminal Injuries Compensation Authority, Whittington House, 19/30 Alfred Place, London WC1E 7LG; 0171 936 3476

Complaints concerning the police can be made to the Police Complaints Authority, 10 Great George Street, London SW1P 3AE; 0171 273 6403

Companies

Records of companies are kept at Companies' House, Crown Way, Cardiff CF4 3UZ; 01222 380801

Searches can be carried out for details of companies and their directors and shareholders. All companies must file accounts annually, which are open to public inspection.

Resolving disputes

Details of local courts can be obtained from local telephone directories and public libraries.

Disputes can also be settled by various industry bodies, for example in the travel trade, ABTA or through trade unions. In addition various other bodies offer mediation services (see page 57 for family mediation), including the following:

The Centre for Dispute Resolution, 100 Fetter Lane, London EC4A 1DD; 0171 430 1852

ACAS, the Advisory, Conciliation and Arbitration Service, 27 Wilton Street, London SW1X 7AZ; 0171 210 3000

The Chartered Institute of Arbitrators will appoint formal arbitrators for commercial disputes – International Arbitration Centre, 24 Angel Gate, City Road, London EC1V 2RS; 0171 837 4483

Trade Union details can be obtained from the Trades Union Congress, Congress House, Great Russell Street, London WC1 3LS; 0171 636 4030

For employment disputes, details concerning industrial tribunals can be obtained from the Industrial Tribunals Enquiry Line 0345 959 775

Legal agreements

When drawing up legal agreements, wills, tenancies etc various forms are published by law stationers such as Oyez, 144–146 Fetter Lane, London EC4; 0171 405 2847 and Stat Plus PLC, who produce a free *Law Forms Directory*, listing forms in most legal areas which are available from Stat Plus, Oyez, the Law Society, Legal Aid Offices and the Courts. Stat Plus House, Greenlea Park, Prince George's Road, London SW19 2PU; 0181 646 5500

Will forms are also available from some big stationery chains such as W H Smith.

Author's firm: Singletons, Eagle House, 67 Brooke Avenue, Harrow, Middlesex HA2 0ND; 0181 864 0835; fax 0181 248 3810; e-mail essingleton@link.org for commercial/business law advice.

Further reading from Kogan Page

Don't Get Mad. Write!, Bruce West, 1993

Going Freelance, 4th Edition, Godfrey Golzen, 1993

Your Employment Rights, Michael Malone, 1992

How to Write a Will and Gain Probate, 4th Edition, Marlene Garsia, 1993

Splitting Up, 2nd Edition, David Green, 1992

Tax Facts, 1994 Edition, Kidsons Impey, 1994

Index